don't
sing happy
birthday

plus
Parenting
Strategies
& Tips

don't
sing happy
birthday

a mother's journey through autism and epilepsy

JONI BROWN

ILLUMIFY
MEDIA.COM
LET'S BRING YOUR BOOK TO LIFE!

Don't Sing Happy Birthday

Published by
Illumify Media Global
www.IllumifyMedia.com
"Let's bring your book to life!"

&

Joni Brown
Joni-Brown.com

Paperback ISBN: 978-1-959099-57-4

Cover design by Eric Brown
Family photographer Lara Mark, LaraMarkPhotography.com

Printed in the United States of America

To Eric,
every step of the way in this special life
you are my navigator, my rationalizer, my punching bag.
Thank you for your above and beyond support.

To Allie,
you have been my favorite teacher.
Thank you for teaching me inner strength, perseverance
and a special love that I never thought I would experience.

To Bingham,
you amaze me every day.
You are my beating heart that walks around this earth.
Thank you for making me laugh when I need to.

disclaimer

The information provided in this book is for general informational purposes only and is not intended to be a substitute for professional medical advice, diagnosis, or treatment. Always seek the advice of your physician or other qualified healthcare provider with any questions you may have regarding a medical condition or treatment for your child and yourself.

Some of the names have been changed to protect their identities, except for the author's immediate family members.

A Mother's Ode to a Life that's Special

If I had to say it quick and well,
Our story's told in a funny nutshell,
Of doctors, hospitals, and tests galore,
And a child who needs a little more.

Through comorbidities and diagnoses we fight,
But we find humor to make it all right,
And though the journey is bumpy and rough,
We stick together and it's enough.

So come and join our little crew,
We'll share our laughs and tears with you,
And in this funny nutshell you'll see,
A community of love and empathy.

Contents

Author's Note

t was the foreign land of parenting. A kind of hidden unspoken world. A 360-degree turn into my first-time parenting arena.

I didn't know the language. Nothing.

- Respite
- Applied Behavior Analysis (ABA)

- Developmental Disabilities (DD)
- Intellectual Disabilities (ID)
- Autism Spectrum Disorder (ASD)
- Individualized Education Program (IEP)
- Assistive Technology

- Adaptive
- Augmentative and Alternative Communication (AAC)
- Sensory Integration

- Behavioral Interventions

- Social Skills Training

- Transition Services

However, I did know these words:

Advocacy.

Empowerment.

Inclusive.

Those words became my focus for my little girl.

This is my story. Our story.

My aim with this book is to offer insights and encouragement to parents of children with special needs who might be struggling to find their purpose and support. With resilience and encouragement, you too can navigate the unique journey of parenting a child with extra needs.

Writing this book was challenging and therapeutic. Emotionally, it forced me to confront memories and experiences that I never wanted to relive. Although I've spent years getting it all down on paper, I had been unknowingly writing this book in my mind since my daughter Allie had her first seizure in 2004 at sixteen months old. Every moment of pain, fear, and hope that followed became forever engraved in my mind.

Writing has become my therapy after I had exhausted all other options. A kind of treatment that has allowed me to reflect in a quiet space when my world was falling apart and the overwhelm was caving in. The writing process allowed me to clarify my and Allie's struggles through my keyboard, typing my heartaches, personal hell, and joyful moments as the roller coaster of memories rolled toward me.

I shaped my writing therapy sessions into *Don't Sing Happy Birthday* with the hope to extend a helping hand to other parents who face the challenges of caring for a child with special needs.

Don't Sing Happy Birthday is a gift for you. . . and your family.

It's two books in one. The first part is my truth-telling, a memoir of a life resembling a perfectly decorated cupcake turned upside down, still beautiful but different. The cupcake is decorated with a sparkler of a candle, which mirrors a seizure in the brain. My life since my daughter's birth hasn't been easy. I recall my personal experiences and stories about Allie's medical challenges that flipped ours upside down. I made a conscious effort to include both the difficult and uplifting moments. Stories from my unexpected life, of how it changed and morphed into something different than I planned.

In addition to my memoir revealed in Part 1, Part 2 is designed to provide you with practical advice and helpful suggestions that can support you through the challenges of caring for a child with disabilities. The type of info that I wish I had at my fingertips when Allie was young.

By shifting your mindset and becoming a strong advocate, you can better navigate parenting and caretaker obstacles that may arise. Think of this section as a tool guide that you can refer to whenever you face difficult situations.

Everyone's journey is different, and you may not be ready to hear everything at once. My hope is that you can find value in the information provided and use it to empower yourself to be the best possible advocate for your child.

I wish I had taken time when I was struggling so long ago to read a book written from a parent's perspective, a parent who had faced many of the challenges and frustrations that I faced on a daily basis. After Allie had her first seizure, it was a fight to get through each day of seizures and medications, on top of multiple doctor and therapy appointments. Being overwhelmed and exhausted was my routine. Seeking therapy or reading a book was the last thing on my mind. It's not that books weren't available to me—they were. Plenty of them. I just wasn't available to them. And I had no one in my circle that said, "Joni, here's what helped guide me through what you are experiencing."

Back then, I was not in the right state of mind to take the time to read or even listen to an audiobook. I was in survival mode. Looking back, I realize that I should have.

Today, I take comfort in learning from those who have walked the caregiver path before me and faced similar challenges. I continue to meet regularly with other parents, attend support groups, read books, and listen to podcasts related to this lifestyle that my family and I are immersed in.

The insights and wisdom shared by others on this topic have proven to be an invaluable resource when navigating my own life. While I was a bit blindsided by all that had brought a tsunami toward me, you don't have to be. It's why I've shared my story in two parts.

PART ONE

Unexpected Life

1
My Life-Changing Moment

My husband Eric and I met in college in 1998. After a year of courtship, we married in a small venue with fifty guests. Both career-driven hard workers with lively social lives, we built a new house and excitedly planned for a family someday. Four years and one

Horror enveloped my body and mind.

"try" later, we became pregnant. It was a textbook pregnancy; everything went as expected. On August 18, 2003, our daughter Allie arrived on time without complications. It was the perfect birth story.

As new parents, we gushed over our gorgeous baby girl. In the next fifteen months, Allie grew up perfectly, hitting all her developmental milestones. Her vocabulary developed quickly, her gross motor skills were right on track, and surprisingly, potty training was a breeze. Her appetite was strong, and she grew tall and healthy. Allie stole the show and our hearts with her outgoing, spunky personality.

We were overjoyed with her, our perfect daughter, and our perfect life.

Allie's toddler days were filled with dancing, singing, tumbling, bouncing, running, and learning all she could as we watched in awe and wonder. Nothing was out of the ordinary in our suburban home. We excitedly built our second house in Sartell, Minnesota, the next town over. Our backyard was a hit with the neighbors, as it was equipped with a giant playset, trampoline, firepit for s'mores, and a small fishing pond. We had it all—health, full social life, job security, and each other.

Then, on December 4, 2004, everything changed.

Everything.

That December evening, I turned on the holiday lights and watched Allie sitting on the floor looking up at the Christmas tree as I made dinner in the kitchen. I walked over to her, wondering what she was staring at so intently. I sat down cross-legged to join her and guide her head to gently rest on my legs. But when I looked down at her sweet face, I quickly realized that something was wrong.

Horror enveloped my body and mind.

Allie's eyes were motionless and wide open. Her pupils dilated and she continued to stare upward without blinking. She began to gasp for breaths, and her body stiffened. Her quick, shallow gasps for air were followed by sounds of saliva gurgling at the back of her tiny throat. Her little face and lips started to turn bluish-purple. *Oh my God. . . my little girl is dying in my lap.*

A blood-curdling scream, "HELP!" hurled out of my mouth to Eric, who was working upstairs in his office. I screamed like I had never screamed before. After a few minutes, she came out of it but was in a confused, sluggish state. Then all became quiet, and she fell asleep in my arms.

Eric called the paramedics, and they arrived shortly after. The EMT told me in a calm voice that Allie most likely experienced a febrile seizure, which is very common in toddlers.

What a simple explanation. But Allie had not been sick, so what was this?

Unfortunately, febrile seizures were not the diagnosis.

Far from it.

Our little girl had a seizure. *What is wrong with her?*

The EMT unit drove away. An hour later she experienced a second seizure, so we packed up the car and headed to the hospital, where she was admitted to the third floor. She then had more than twelve seizures throughout the night—cluster seizures, one after the other, in two- to three-minute episodes that came every forty-five minutes.

Allie was monitored closely and supplied with an oxygen mask over her tiny face. All night, multiple doctors and nurses threaded in and out till the morning. All involved were perplexed, and nobody could find a way to control the seizures. They gave us the option to have her airlifted to Children's Minnesota Hospital in Minneapolis. Of course, we accepted.

Allie was unconscious during the helicopter ride. Our orders were clear: one parent travels with Allie in the helicopter. Eric went back home to pack bags and met us after his hour-long drive to the hospital. After we landed, she was admitted to the Pediatric Intensive Care Unit (PICU). The PICU staff had been alerted that she was on her way and were waiting and ready to begin her care and treatment. This was the first of our seven-day stay.

Doctors worked through the hours and finally calmed Allie's seizures with heavy doses of drugs through the IV inserted into her tiny vein. Then they swiftly diagnosed her: epilepsy. Her brain was broken and so were we. The questions we had were countless, including:

> *What caused her seizures?*
>
> *Will she have more?*
>
> *When can we leave the hospital and take her home?*

Our perfect world had been transformed in an instant by that one seizure under the Christmas lights only twenty-four hours earlier. It was an awful experience for our small family, and I was unprepared for the emotional pain and suffering that was to come. On the second day of Allie's hospital stay, Eric and I sat down exhausted from the massive stress and the bottomless mugs of coffee we had consumed. In a small break room on a wobbly round laminate table, we talked about the sense of loss we were both feeling.

"She's my little buddy," he told me. His eyes welled to the brim as he spoke.

We grieved in that tiny break room for the loss of the child that she was *supposed* to be. How could this have happened to her? To us? The beginning of an entire new world felt like it had suddenly fallen upon us. I felt completely disconnected from reality and unable to comprehend what was happening.

On the seventh day we got the green light to take Allie home. We had little guidance going forward. The instructions during discharge were to fill the medication as soon as possible and take a sleep apnea monitor home for Allie to wear at night. Nothing more. Not a detailed step by step of how to take care of her and her seizures. I was exhausted and all I could think of was getting Allie back home into her comfy bedroom. That was my focus. I accepted the orders, and we were discharged.

An empty feeling surrounded me when we got home as the house was eerily quiet. I sat down and read through Allie's discharge papers. It clearly stated her diagnosis of epilepsy. I also found a three-fold brochure titled "Epilepsy" tucked in between the papers. In that moment, it sunk in that this was Allie's official diagnosis.

For a week I believed she was experiencing an acute condition—something that would subside and go away, a fluke. It hadn't crossed my mind until that moment to think this was a chronic condition that would last forever.

It was too much to accept. I felt a heavy weight the size of a bowling ball sitting on my chest. I knew in that moment life would never be the same. My tears did not stop flowing for days.

One Day at a Time

To say that the first few weeks at home after our hospital stay were unkind is an under-statement. We now had a name for what was happening to Allie so we could mentally move forward. Phenobarbital, a tried-and-true medication for seizure control, was flowing through her sixteen-month-old bloodstream. It was unbearable to think about her tiny pure body being flooded with medicine.

We became functional zombies.

The sleep monitor Allie's doctor had ordered her was to prevent Sudden Unexpected Death in Epilepsy, or SUDEP, in which a person with epilepsy dies suddenly and unexpectedly, with no clear cause of death identified during an autopsy. Allie's chances of meeting such a fate were high, as it's estimated to occur in approximately 1 in 1,000 people per year who are diagnosed with epilepsy.

Nighttime became a nightmare for us, in which none of us could sleep for more than an hour on any night. The sleep apnea monitor was belted around Allie's chest and lung area to detect any pause in respirations, so should Allie cease to breathe or experience a seizure, a loud alarm would be triggered. Because of its inaccuracy, the apnea monitor alarm would consistently trigger multiple times each night. Eric and I were exhausted by our new routine. We became functional zombies.

During daytime, we needed to administer medications to Allie to control her seizures three times each day. She was prescribed liquid drugs because of her young age, but Eric and I were not formally trained in how to properly administer them to a very active and temperamental toddler, so the first time we had to administer the phenobarbital was a disaster. We pulled the medicine up through a syringe, then we held her down and squirted the shots into her mouth. But Allie wasn't thrilled. She thrashed her head back and forth so hard that her mouth didn't catch the medicine—her cheeks, ears, neck, and hair did. We were horrified—as well as tired, stressed, and clueless about what we should have done instead. Allie's sweet face was now a reddish orange color from our ineffective delivery of her meds. What a shitshow we were living in.

All the staff at Children's Minnesota had said to us when we left was *Good luck to you*. They didn't disclose anything we needed to know to care for Allie, such as what to expect when we got home, or how meds should be given to a toddler, or the side effects of the medications. Eric and I had to fast-forward our learning curve. We created and put into play our own shoot-from-the-hip crash course.

We knew she needed her medicines and didn't want a repeat of the *syringegate* incident. None of the meds tasted good to a toddler. We became endlessly creative in administering them, and we mastered it well by burying the awful-tasting medicines in a variety of foods, such as applesauce, milkshakes, ice cream, bananas, and smoothies.

The goal: get meds into Allie's system.

We smashed that goal.

Even though we had our triumphs, our days were hard. We were now living a life we had neither expected nor envisioned. Where most parents were marveling at the speedy mental and physical growth of their children, we no longer did. Allie wasn't growing quickly anymore. Each day, we counted seizures, or lack thereof, and sadly waited for the next cluster to hit. Temper tantrums and horrible behaviors became a daily occurrence. These new behaviors were a direct result of the side effects from her anti-seizure drugs.

With the new stress and anxiety that surrounded us, Eric and I had no choice but to forge on. Day after day we slowly accepted the unexpected life that was here to stay and learned together how to manage temper tantrums. Before outings, we verbally front-loaded her, preparing her for what was happening with clear, simple words of expectations and timelines. Special tactics were the order of the day. Bribery was a result of our defeat to give in when we did not have *it* in us to argue during a tantrum. Snacks and toys were her valued bribe, and it worked. With time and practice, we became more comfortable and capable of working together as a family through this transitional time and grew more confident in our ability as parents to tackle any challenge together, to survive this new kind of parenting, and to keep Allie healthy.

Allie's seizures became better controlled with minor medication changes. I resumed my career as the marketing director for a new home builder while Eric fulfilled the dual role of work-at-home computer programmer and stay-at-home dad. Since Allie loved socializing with other children, Eric found a nearby neighbor with a small in-home daycare which Allie happily attended part-time. It was a great fit.

On my first day back to the office, the company's CFO brought me into a tiny conference room. She was a friend of mine. . . or so I'd thought. She wasn't happy with me and expressed how I had failed to reach out to the company about my absence while in the hospital with Allie. I felt depleted as I sat across from her, defending my actions in my head in a mindless rant.

I had a sudden medical emergency. I had not planned on a helicopter medical flight for Allie or a hospital stay. And I didn't know whether any company protocol existed to follow. I'd had no clue how to respond during a family crisis, especially when I had been out of my mind.

The CFO told me that my poor communication would go in my file to be considered at my next review. I was taken aback and wanted to run to the bathroom and hide, but I quietly stayed seated and took the punishment without emotion until she was done with her stoic lecture.

Those days in the hospital with Allie had consumed every bit of my energy, and I left the room deflated, with nothing left to fight back or argue. I thought, *How can this mother of two be so cold and unempathetic?* After all, just a few months earlier I had been swimming in her backyard pool with her children. The way she had lectured me was harsh, and I took it personally. Looking back, I should have made a quick phone call to my boss and explained my family crises or at minimum had a family member communicate to my company on my behalf.

I became melancholy from that point on while working for that company, and my friendship with the CFO ended that day in that conference room. With my mind no longer at work but instead focused on my new role of keeping my child alive, the job became the least of my concerns. But the insurance benefits were good for our family, so I forged on working my 9–5.

When the Great Recession hit in 2008, my company was forced to lay off roughly 80 percent of its workforce. *Could this be the calm within my turbulent storm?* When most of the population were terrified and in a financial crisis of losing so much, I took on a different perspective. My layoff turned into an opportunity to stay at home and concentrate on raising Allie. We were fortunate that Eric's job provided nicely for our family unit. My mind was content, and I was focused *at* my new role.

Embracing Change as a Stay-at-Home Mom to a Child with Extra Needs

The timing was perfect during the recession to be a stay-at-home mom. Allie was now four years old. She and I filled our days with playgrounds, swimming pools, visiting libraries, and of course attending endless doctor appointments. I tackled responsibilities for Allie that required extra time, care, and training

Will she ever get a break? Will I?

like a pro. I became hyper focused on surviving the day-to-day challenges such as feeding, seizure watching, calming large temper tantrums, and figuring out her ever-changing behaviors.

One duty that took me by surprise was her time-consuming medication management. Allie was getting older, and her body was changing and having more breakthrough seizures. For better seizure control, we needed to increase medications, which were now in pill form—no more liquid medicines to hide in smoothies. Allie swallowed large pills better than most adults could. Drug failures led to new prescriptions, which meant many trips to the local drive-through pharmacies and back-and-forth communications with doctors and nurses.

I worked closely with her epileptologist, diving into the complex process of finding the right combination of drugs at the right therapeutic levels to control Allie's seizures. She underwent blood tests to ensure she was receiving the appropriate dose to prevent seizures without causing harm or major side effects. This included sixty-day liver-function tests and periodic blood counts for certain anti-epileptic drugs. Thankfully, Allie didn't mind getting her blood drawn. I'm grateful for that.

"Are you going to use the butterfly needle?" Allie asked the nurse one day at a lab appointment. "Yes, I am. . . you are my favorite patient, Allie Brown!" the kind nurse replied. At a sweet age of four-and-a-half years, she was mature as a seasoned patient for any nurse or doctor because of her exposure to the medical arena at such a young age.

Medication Mayhem

Allie continued to experience severe behavioral side effects from the pharmaceutical drugs. I was completely uneducated in how the drugs were impacting her behavior. Mood swings, rages, and irritability were a constant. She had giant temper tantrums during the simple transition from car to inside the house, an event that consisted of twenty minutes of screaming, refusals from every angle, and tears from both of us.

On top of that, the drugs made her drowsy during the day and restless at night. My alarm clock was never used because Allie rose before sunrise; therefore, I too rose. Coffee could not come fast enough in those early dark mornings. By 9:00 a.m., I was a walking zombie, trying to gain energy to entertain my highly spirited cherub through the rest of the long day. Then repeat. I was in a constant state of mommy mayhem.

My tired mind wondered:

Is she just a temperamental and energetic kid?
What anti-seizure drugs do not create bad behaviors?
Is there a bigger neurological disorder?
What am I missing?

Her physicians failed to fully educate me on the medications' horrible side effects on Allie, nor was I in the right head space to question them about how medications negatively affected behavior. In hindsight, I didn't need them to tell me what I already knew. And, with looming school days ahead, I needed to figure this out.

Will she ever get a break? Will I?

We tried other AEDs (anti-epileptic drugs) but to no avail; the seizures came without warning. On top of that, her body was growing, and she presented with an odd new behavior. At night in her bed before falling asleep, she constantly banged her head up and down on her pillow while making a humming sound. She sounded like a fire engine. The repetitive motion of head-banging seemed to give her some comfort and relief after a long day. (I later understood this activity as *stimming*, which acts as a self-soothing mechanism for many people with autism).

To put it mildly, my stay-at-home mom gig was utterly draining.

Adaptive Sports: My Lifesaver

My motto: *In between seizure clusters, we live life to its fullest.*

Allie was joyful, without fear, and I was her number-one cheerleader. Her personality was larger than life, and we had no intentions of holding her back. "Mom, Mom, I wanna wear a pink tutu and I wanna spin around."

I signed her up for a dance class at a local dance studio. Instead of dancing in a line like all the other ballerinas, Allie spun and tumbled around the entire room, all while admiring herself as she moved in front of the full-length mirrors at every angle. She twisted and twirled without any cares in the world. My heart was warmed because she was so happy living her best life.

Unfortunately, not everyone shared my delight. The other children and their parents glared in disapproval. The dance instructor did not fully appreciate how spirited Allie was either, as she could not control the unrestrained dancing enthusiast in her own studio.

Noticing a continued disruptive pattern Allie was creating during dance lessons, the instructor pulled me aside after class. With a soft smile, she handed me a tri-fold pamphlet titled, "Adaptive Recreation." She kindly explained that Allie would be a better fit in an adaptive dance lesson offered at the local community center. I understood her guidance and thanked her as Allie and I walked out of that charming dance studio for the last time.

Adaptive recreation, a.k.a. adaptive rec, refers to recreational activities and programs that are specifically designed or modified to accommodate individuals with disabilities, enabling their participation and enjoyment.

Just the word alone—*adaptive*—was the perfect no-pressure kind of word for my spirited tiny dancer. Prior to learning about adaptive rec, I had been unaware of its existence. I quickly came to appreciate the modified activities for children with extra needs who want to play sports and participate in fun class offerings. These programs are sometimes also referred to as therapeutic recreation, leisure, or activity therapy. Throughout the year, our local parks and recreation department offered adaptive arts and crafts, soccer, tennis, rock climbing, and swimming classes. These were a welcome group of activities to fulfill our sensory-seeking Allie.

I had the time, and Allie had the energy.

Allie loved the variety of classes I signed her up for. They allowed her to stay engaged and active, while also meeting her unique needs. There was no need to hide her defiant behaviors and bouncy ways. At each activity, like-minded parents were on the same journey I was. I felt relaxed and at home in good company. We sat on the sidelines watching our sensory-seeking children run and play out their energy. It was a win-win all around.

Special Olympics was another great find for Allie's social and physical well-being. The organization prides itself on providing year-round sports for children and adults with disabilities. They focus on what athletes "*can* do, not what they can't do." When participating, we never had to worry about how she looked or acted. This community understood if she had a meltdown. This was my kind of community.

In Special Olympics soccer, Allie was adamant about only playing goalie. If the coach placed her on the main field, she would pout, kick, and pull out clumps of grass from the field until she was made goalie. Eric and I both knew as we drove her to practices that we had to preload her with encouragement to try other positions. She eventually stopped having fits and played all positions.

Other activities Allie tried through Special Olympics were bowling, tennis, basketball, bocce ball (her favorite), and swimming. The nominal activity fees for both adaptive recreation and Special Olympics didn't completely break the bank. The programs are often subsidized, allowing participants to play for a reduced fee and sometimes at no cost. Another win-win.

2

Rapidly Educated in Autism

ive-year-old Allie began attending kindergarten at our local
public elementary school in the fall of 2008. Her school days
became my respite. I could take a walk without interruption
and clear my mind for a few hours, but my respite was short lived
some days. Allie began
experiencing an increase in
seizures. They were occurring
every four to five weeks. When
her seizure clusters came during the early morning hours, that
meant no school and me tending to her medical needs for the next
twenty-four hours. Then repeat.

Some of my *whys* had been answered.

Despite our attempts at calming her increasing behavior issues,
she still struggled with regulation. And no official diagnosis except
epilepsy was in her school paperwork. A month into the school
year, we received a call from her school's office to come in to talk

to the principal about Allie's behavior issues in the classroom. As we sat down, the principal informed us of how disruptive our daughter had been in class.

"The teacher is reporting that Allie moves around during circle time. She doesn't sit well at her desk, and I am noticing social communication difficulties with other students. Today, I witnessed her pushing another student on the playground."

We were not surprised, as a week ago we had heard a similar story directly from her kindergarten teacher.

Then a bombshell came out of the principal's mouth: "If the aggressive behaviors persist, it may become grounds for expulsion."

My blood pressure rose, making my head red and hot. I immediately became defensive. "Wait, what? Expelled? On what grounds? Because a five-year-old can't control some mild behaviors?"

The next words that came out of her mouth were truly disheartening. "On the grounds of bullying."

I was stunned to hear such a shocking word about my daughter. I asked, "A kindergartener can get expelled for bullying? At that age, do they even understand what that is? Because the concept is not in Allie's realm of thinking and actually far from it."

She continued, "We have a zero-tolerance bullying policy."

I replied, "As you should! But my child has brain issues and different challenges; she has epilepsy!"

"I understand that your daughter has special needs; however, without any other diagnosis, we could expel her if this continues," the principal replied. "I'm suggesting you get something in writing from a specialist. In the meantime, the school will proceed with testing and bring in a special education team, along with starting her on an IEP to get Allie the support she needs." The principal in her own roundabout way absolutely knew and witnessed with her experience that Allie had a lot more than just epilepsy, and she needed something in writing to protect the school and Allie.

Those words were foreign to me. *My daughter needs to be in special education classes? And what the hell is an IEP?* I was so naive and undereducated in special needs education.

Eric and I drove away, frustrated. We now understood the significance of another formal diagnosis within the realm of public education. The principal was helping us, but in the heat of the moment I didn't see that. A measly piece of paper with words describing and labeling Allie, because apparently epilepsy was not enough to protect her. We were both frustrated and saddened by the situation. It was clear that obtaining a diagnosis was necessary if we wanted Allie to attend public schools. I got right to work. Sought out a psychologist and was placed on an eight-month waitlist to get Allie tested. Kindergarten was a blur and full of messy mommy emotions the entire school year.

Understanding an Autism Diagnosis

Over a four-day period in May 2009, a psychologist administered an Autism Diagnostic Assessment to test Allie for autism. Afterward, Eric and I sat in front of a desk in a stale, tiny office in the basement of a medical complex while she presented her conclusions. Allie was diagnosed with autism. The psychologist typed up a nine-page report on her findings, and in black-and-white print, her official diagnosis was Asperger's syndrome. It included an explanation of why the diagnosis was justified. Then she reached into her drawer and handed us a five-page printout of resources available within the autism community. Eric and I left her office, looked at each other, silently shrugged our shoulders, and drove away.

Allie was protected now from being expelled with that official diagnosis in hand and delivered to her school. Thanks to her diagnosis of autism, an IEP was now in place. Allie was able to access district therapy services and the staff support she needed to succeed in the classroom. More about IEPs later in the book.

When you hear the term *autism*, what comes to mind? You might think of quirky behaviors, atypical traits, challenges with eye contact, high intelligence, kindness, and creativity. Individuals with autism exhibit a wide array of characteristics, with their brains operating in distinctive manners, so each person on the spectrum is truly unique.

Autism spectrum disorder (ASD) is a condition that impacts communication, social interaction, and behavior, stemming from neurological and developmental factors. It's characterized by a wide range of symptoms and levels of impairment and is typically diagnosed in early childhood.

The Centers for Disease Control and Prevention 2023 data reveals that around 1 in 36 children in the U.S. have been diagnosed with ASD, with boys being four times more likely to receive a diagnosis compared to girls.

In 2013, Asperger's syndrome, Allie's diagnosis, was incorporated under the diagnosis of ASD in the fifth edition of the Diagnostic and Statistical Manual of Mental Disorders (DSM-5), which is used by mental health professionals to diagnose autism and other developmental disorders.

Today, more parents and healthcare professionals are aware that the prevalence of autism has risen to epidemic levels. They are more knowledgeable about the signs and symptoms, which ultimately leads to earlier diagnoses. Early intervention and support can improve outcomes for children with autism. I am glad that an increase in public awareness is leading more parents to seek out evaluations for their children at younger ages as we did for Allie.

Of Course, We Knew

Early on, the signs of autism were there. My mind never wanted to go there.

At nine months old, she broke her plastic highchair by repeatedly rocking back too hard while she waited for her lunch in the kitchen. I asked the pediatrician at a wellness visit about the incident.

"Allie is strong and advanced. She is perfectly normal," she replied.

I was confused by the doctor's quick and unconcerned answer. *Breaking a highchair is normal for a nine-month-old baby? No, that's not right,* I thought to myself as I drove home.

Over the next two years, I slowly began to realize that Allie was indeed displaying more than just epilepsy. Subtle behavioral clues surfaced, like her fearlessness in dangerous situations, lack of interest in playing with others, repetitive behaviors, sensory sensitivities, and an inability to sit still. Autism floated in my mind a few times, but I was hoping it wasn't the "A" word. My naive mind thought, *It's just sensory intolerance.*

My mommy suspicions of autism were validated. Many years prior, when Allie rocked in her highchair till it broke, it was now crystal clear that she had been stimming, a common behavior observed in individuals with autism. Stimming can include a wide range of repetitive behaviors or movements, such as hand-flapping, rocking, spinning, twirling, finger-flicking, tapping, or repeating sounds or words. It can help regulate sensory input, relieve anxiety, or serve as a self-soothing mechanism.

Soon after the diagnosis, I noticed Allie rocking for the first time in a public library. While sitting crisscross, she rocked back and forth in the middle of a crowded children's story room. I understood her urge to calm herself, as it was very loud with many kids chattering. Another stimming activity she performed was nightly spinning around in our living room. Her repetitive behavior calmed her down after hectic days.

We never felt that the ASD label changed her or how we intended to raise her. *Allie is just Allie.*

Applied Behavior Analysis (ABA) Therapy

Allie's behaviors were not for the weak. Eric and I were always on high alert. In addition to head-banging and biting her arm when frustrated, she would hit and kick us if we got too close during her emotional outbursts. We had to learn techniques to safely immobilize her by wrapping our legs and arms around her in hopes of soothing and calming her. Living through hours of her emotional storms was painful and exhausting for us both.

At times, Allie's fits of anger became extremely unmanageable. Now at age seven, she was bigger and stronger. During one of her meltdowns, Allie pulled pictures and decorations off her bedroom walls and shelves. Afraid that she might seriously hurt herself, we stripped down her beautifully decorated bedroom to a bare minimum and stored away her clothes in our bedroom closet.

Her clothing hangers, gone. Her shelves stored away. Her dresser and nightstand went into the garage.

Only her mattress, bedding, pillows, and stuffed animals were allowed. She now had a soft place to rage. What else could we do? We felt hopeless.

On top of these outbursts, we constantly reminded her how to behave, but nothing was sticking.

Allie, close the bathroom door when you're on the toilet.

Allie, you can't just run out of the classroom.

Allie, please calm down.

You have your answer! No is no.

We felt defeated as parents. We were sad, and physically and mentally exhausted daily. Seeing no end to the constant suffering, we knew we absolutely needed professional help. Internet searches became a midnight norm for me. I barreled down the Google rabbit hole into the autism therapy world. Asking questions in support groups, soaking up other parents' feedback and resources as to what therapies helped and which ones failed. Parents know; they lived it and live it.

After researching specifically for behavioral therapies, Applied Behavior Analysis (ABA) sounded like the best fit. A trained professional took the lead to help with Allie's behaviors. Kelly, a Board-Certified Behavior Analyst (BCBA), came to our home to study Allie's behaviors in our environment. She collected data and created a therapy plan by setting, measuring, and preparing her goals for Allie.

Finally, the weight lifted off Eric and me. A beacon of hope named Kelly walked through our front door. We finally had the help we had been desperately needing.

Some of the specific goals Kelly created for Allie were:

- Improving Allie's emotional regulation and coping skills

- Developing play skills, such as turn-taking and sharing

- Closing the bathroom door when toileting

- Reducing fleeing behaviors

Kelly developed a behavior intervention plan (BIP) that outlined these goals and strategies for Allie's entire course of treatment. The BIP included a detailed description of Allie's behavior, the target behavior for change, the strategies to be used to promote the desired behavior, and how the progress would be monitored and evaluated over time.

Kelly performed intensive weekly ABA sessions with Allie in our home with a set time commitment. I pulled Allie out of school, and her teacher agreed to the therapy sessions. Addressing behaviors came first, then successful classroom academics could follow.

Allie made significant progress with ABA therapy. One of the targeted goals was to change her negative reaction to the word *no*. Kelly used a gradual approach to help her become more comfortable with hearing the word *no*. They started with simple requests or situations where Allie was more likely to accept a "no" answer, then gradually increased the complexity or difficulty of the situation. Through this repetitive, sometimes boring exposure, Allie developed the skills to accept "no" in more challenging situations.

Kelly also used this gradual approach to help Allie become more comfortable coping with negative emotions. She used a *Candy Land* board game to demonstrate the concept of losing and how to cope with the negative feelings that can come with it. They started with simple situations where Allie was more likely to accept losing and gradually increased the difficulty of the game. Through consistent practice, Allie made great strides in her emotional development. She was better able to handle losing, and eventually, other negative emotions she experienced in daily activities. Kelly tailored the approach to her individual needs and provided support and guidance along the way.

I had initially been skeptical about whether ABA therapy would be effective. A huge time commitment was required of both Allie and me. But after I became educated in the pros and cons, I understood its potential benefits.

The entire family needs to make a solid commitment to it. And we did. ABA therapy has its limitations, as do most therapies. What works for one child may not work for another. ABA is structured around rules. Allie had an advantage; she was a natural rule abider. The black-and-white structured approach worked well for her, and it was a huge benefit. Eric and I finally felt relief in our home.

Allie underwent three cumulative years of ABA therapy throughout her childhood, receiving separate specific treatments during her elementary, middle, and high school years. These sessions fine-tuned Allie's emotional regulation and coping skills during her different stages of development. This helped her to socially mature and manage her behavior with fewer eloping (leaving a safe or supervised space without permission or warning) rages and displays of defiance. ABA was not a cure-all, but it provided enough relief to improve Allie's quality of life. We healed our emotional scars as a family as well.

The Day I Fired Allie's Doctor

Over the years, Allie's seizure medication was changed a dozen times. She took many different cocktails of anti-epileptic seizure meds, or AEDs, which all brought nasty side effects. Allie was a very kind and sweet girl when the medication mix was right.

However, some meds made her very aggressive and self-injurious.

I had been a raging mama bear, attacking anything in my path to get answers.

At seven years old, her pediatric psychiatrist prescribed a popular antipsychotic medication. Shortly after, I saw an alarming mood change in our sweet girl. It was during a move into a new house. Adjusting to the surroundings is challenging no matter what. One day, we had planned to check out the local park, but then plans changed because I needed to wait for the internet and cable man to hook up our new service. I delivered the message to Allie with a deep breath, knowing her wrath would follow. "I am so sorry. We will go to the park later, Allie." Allie was not happy.

With a growl, her crying turned quickly into a raging fit, and she bit off a large corner of our new living room wall. I watched her red face pull away the sheetrock, screaming while the white powdery chunks fell onto her shirt, down to her feet, and onto the floor. Her mouth was full of slobbery sheetrock as tears streamed down her beet-red face.

I assumed that too many changes at once led to her frustrations. At that moment, I was not mad at her, but *I felt so sad for her.* She must have felt sad on the inside to commit that dramatic act of rage.

I went to the kitchen and brought her some warm washcloths to help her clean up. I knew she needed a distraction. "Allie, there's a new stuffed animal in your bedroom the neighbor dropped off. Let's go see that." We went upstairs and grabbed her new fluffy toy.

A bubble bath was next in my toolbox of ideas. The warm water was welcomed and calmed her soul. The next day, I phoned the psychiatrist and told her about Allie's mental status.

"That medication should be a mood stabilizer," the psychiatrist replied.

"Well, it's doing the opposite for her! She's crawling out of her skin!" I said.

The psychiatrist suggested we slowly increase the dosage of the medication.

"Really?" I said. "That's your solution? To put more of this drug into her bloodstream? You are not listening to me!" I shouted. I paused for a brief moment and sharply continued. "You're fired." Then I hung up.

At that moment I knew I had the power to choose other doctors. And I realized that doctors make mistakes.

My heart raced, as I was emotionally upset. The following day I called the Nurseline to get specific directions to safely wean Allie off that drug. We took a long break from psychiatry and psychiatric medications altogether after that. To my surprise, Allie's body and mental state did get better without antipsychotics. Unfortunately, it took much ugly trial and error to figure this out.

The Day Her Doctor Fired *Me*

Can a physician fire a patient? Yes. It happened to me. Generally speaking, physicians, doctors, therapists, etc., are excellent and some will often go above and beyond to help your child. But some fall short.

For seven years I was trapped in a personal hell, with the relentless question spinning in my mind like an insane mama bear of what was wrong with my sweet girl. My investigative mind knew seizures were the result of something *much* larger. The *why* never deserted me. And I refused to Band-Aid and tuck it away. If we found the cause, then maybe we could cure her.

I used Allie's pediatrician, whom I will call Dr. Shew for the purpose of protecting her identity, as my investigative assistant. I pressed her for answers, resources, studies, and testing regarding Allie's complex issues. She went along with my sleuthing for a solid two years. We were discovering clues, trying to decode the mysteries hidden within the complex web of symptoms. I was relentless when it came to demanding labs ordered or a new medication prescribed.

Then one day, I received a voice message from her nurse shortly after a lab appointment.

"Dr. Shew has decided she is no longer a good fit for your daughter. She has referred care to another pediatrician who can better meet your daughter's needs."

I processed about two words of what she said and spit out one word in return. "OK. . . "

"Can I transfer you over to our scheduling department to get you set up for a new patient appointment for Allie?" she went on, pausing to hear my response.

In a millisecond, my neck and face rapidly heated up and turned a dark red. I went quickly into an internal rage. My response was instant rage. "Wait. . . Dr. Shew is not going to see Allie anymore?"

"Correct," she said.

My mama bear unloaded its fury onto the poor nurse. I am not proud of the words that came out. "She can't just quit on us! I have never heard of any doctor who fires a patient! Is this even legal?" I might have thrown out a swear word in my statements.

The nurse was calm and kept repeating that we were no longer a good fit and that we'd be better assisted by another doctor who could handle our needs. The nurse's composure and steadiness during my rant was commendable. Extremely pissed off, and I eventually hung up.

I felt like a defeated victim. Allie was still my medical mystery to solve. I told everyone who would listen *about the terrible doctor who fired me.* In hindsight, it's clear I pushed Dr. Shew for more than she could ever give me. I had been a raging mama bear, attacking anything in my path to get answers. In my obsession to find a clue, a cure, an answer, Dr. Shew was the unfortunate target.

Nevertheless, I have grown from that experience and learned to be a more level-headed mama bear. I now hold more realistic expectations of doctors, appreciating their role in supporting and assisting me.

3

Beating
My Self-Pity

*B*eing a stay-at-home mom is so amazing!
 You are so lucky not to have to hold a 9–5 job!
 What a great life you have!

People say these kinds of things to me all the time, and I smile at them and nod. But what I'd like to say is. . . I am a mother of a child with extra needs. This is no picnic. I watch her horrible seizures and I make sure she doesn't bang her head on a hard floor. I clean up her bloody lips and change her sheets after she loses bladder control. I didn't sign up for this kind of intensity. There. I said it (on paper). I never said it out loud to anyone.

Everyone has their own ugly struggles.

Nevertheless, I strived to maintain a "normal" family life. One afternoon I took Allie to our local park to meet with some neighborhood moms and their kids, where I found myself surrounded by seemingly perfect children playing nicely together. On the sidelines, their flawless mothers discussed their own issues, openly sharing problems like workaholic husbands who didn't help with household chores, their children who constantly argued over the latest video games, and other trivial topics such as interior decorating and their upcoming beach vacations.

I felt out of place. They certainly seemed to have an amazing life! Why were *they* complaining? Embarrassed to admit this, I felt sorry for myself after I left. I wallowed in self-pity and unhealthy thoughts filled with waves of scorn, jealousy, and envy.

Those polished women and their simple problems. Meh. They seriously had no idea how lucky they were.

Their child was healthy.

Their child would drive a car someday.

Their child would leave the nest and live on their own.

My days, however, were consumed by more complicated affairs.

Would I get a solid four-hour stretch of sleep tonight?

When would her seizures come?

Would her new therapist be the right match?

It's not fair, I told myself over and over. I studied some self-care techniques to rid myself of the self-pity and jealousy. Running and walking has been a great outlet. Eric and I went down the meditation and yoga route a few times. For me, what has sustained my self-care journey has been running, reading, then ultimately writing. My running and writing has grown into an introverted self-care therapy that I can do on my own time and pace.

Talking to friends who also are raising children with extra needs was another great way to connect and not feel sorry for myself. I knew I had to do these things, because if I didn't, I would crumble.

I learned to rise above my jealous thoughts toward others. It took years to practice and master. Everyone has their own ugly struggles. It gave me no comfort to keep those dark thoughts and feelings swirling in my mind. I've learned to steer my energy toward much simpler pleasures and small wins. This is a significant personal accomplishment.

A Lesson on the Playground

Despite overcoming my own challenges with others, Allie's public behaviors continued to be difficult. We spent hours at parks and fun playgrounds. Because of her sensitivity to high-sensory situations, Allie preferred a more independent style of play to reduce overwhelming sensory input that her peers did not understand. On top of that, she had no social filter. If someone had bad breath, she told them straight up.

During Allie's elementary years, we lived next to a girl named Leslie who was the same age. On a few occasions, they played together at our neighborhood park. One day, while Allie and Leslie were running up and down the play structure, Allie said to Leslie, "You have chicken legs." I heard it from a distance and thought, *oh shit*. My eyes bulging in fear of what might happen next.

Unfortunately, Leslie's uptight mother overheard the comment and did not take it well.

"That is uncalled for," Leslie's mother spat at me. "I do *not* want my daughter to be subjected to insults like that. We are ending this playdate. Goodbye!"

Bye.

That was it with them. From then on, we became more selective about our friendships. We concentrated on building relationships with people who shared similar backgrounds by connecting with families who also had children with extra needs. Natural friendships formed when Allie participated in adaptive recreation activities. These special friendships were more sustainable and made more sense for our family.

A More Dangerous Lesson

"I am not proud of the moment when I _____." Fill in the blank for yourself. Have you ever experienced a moment as a parent where you felt overwhelmed and emotionally crumbled under pressure? It's a common experience among parents to lose control in heated moments and, upon reflection, don't feel proud of how we handled the situation.

One warm and sunny Tuesday when I was driving Allie home from a biofeedback therapy appointment close to rush hour down a busy highway, unbeknownst to me, eight-year-old Allie unlatched her seatbelt and began to climb out of her booster seat. When I looked in the rearview mirror into the backseat, I was shocked by what I saw.

"Allie, get back in that car seat now!" I said sternly, but she continued climbing out to explore the backseat area.

I said loudly, "Get in your seat and buckle in!" At that point, I needed more ammunition, so every bribe I could think of poured out of my mouth. "Do you want garlic croutons?" They were her all-time favorite snack food, but it didn't seem to work, so I tried another. "Do you want a toy from the toy store? I will stop; it is just right up ahead at the next exit."

Despite my loud attempts to bribe her with junk food and toys, her face appeared void of any response. *What was going on inside her brain?*

Still trying to concentrate on driving in heavy traffic while feeling emotionally overheated, I sternly yelled, "Get back in that car seat, and we will drive to the toy store. If you don't, you won't get anything!"

I felt panicked and distracted, to say the least. No other options came to mind, so I pulled over onto the shoulder of the highway and stopped the car. My parked sedan shook as speeding cars and large semi-trucks zoomed past. I quickly punched on the hazard lights.

At this point, Allie was climbing into the front passenger seat, for what reason, I didn't know. I angrily screamed directly into her small face just an inch from mine. "Get back in your seat!" I was shaking and out of control with pure fear.

I continued pulling out every bribe I could think of.

"Allie, I have a new magical bathtub prize at home upstairs in the bathroom!" I lied. Without a sound, she reversed over the center cup holder and buckled herself safely into her seat. *Hook, line, and sinker.* As soon as I heard that she was clicked into her seat, I cautiously entered my lane and concentrated on the road ahead. Neither of us uttered any words for the next ten minutes. My heart was still racing when I finally came to a stop in the garage and turned off the car.

"Okay, Allie. Let's go get that bag of chips."

"The cheesy ones?" she asked, without a care in the world. She bounced into the house and never asked about the bath surprise.

My body was still shaking from the adrenaline rush. I watched her silently gobble down her chips at our kitchen table. I grabbed my phone and closed myself in the pantry to ugly cry. Even after all she had just put me through, this mama bear still wanted to protect her from seeing my sobs.

She doesn't understand any of it.

I called my sister Jolene, and luckily she picked up. I sobbed into the phone and spoke of the events that had just taken place.

"I feel ashamed and embarrassed. I yelled so hard in her face. Oh my God! She has special needs. What is wrong with me?" I rambled and sobbed.

"You are *not* a bad mother, Joni. You did nothing wrong in that scary situation."

"Okay."

"You safely got her home. Do not feel bad for yelling at her."

"Okay. . . yeah. It's not her fault she did that. Her innocent brain has no sense of fear or danger." I justified her actions as I always did.

"I would have yelled even more if I was in your situation! You are the strongest mother I know, Joni."

Her comforting words brought me back to reason and helped me move on, because I still had to continue with our day, which luckily went without another incident.

I doubt Allie remembered the event. I realized I needed other tactics for that situation. I played different scenarios in my mind, considering what I could have done differently. I should have pulled over at the nearest exit to find a safer option for parking; that would have been a calmer choice. However, in the heat of the moment, my reasoning was nonexistent.

Although that experience occurred many years ago, I still recall it vividly. It was an emotional, traumatic event for me, and even as I write about it now, I find myself becoming emotional and feeling a sense of sadness about what we went through that day. Thankfully, Allie has never done anything that dangerous since.

The Summer I Broke

Teenagers already navigate the challenges of raging hormones and the awkwardness of physical changes. But when you add a neurological disorder with emotional dysregulation

I became the mom that I never wanted to be.

into the mix, as in the case of thirteen-year-old Allie, things become even more difficult.

Some days, Allie would behave appropriately, displaying kindness and politeness in social situations without any outbursts of anger or self-harm. However, the very next day could be the complete opposite, by stomping her feet and threatening to run to the store if I didn't give her a bag of her favorite croutons.

The summer of 2018 was particularly tough, to say the least. The sweet Allie we knew pre-puberty, with excitement and joy in her eyes when she visited parks, swung on monkey bars, and slid down slides, took a new direction. Her attitude became snarky and hit us hard.

Allie was invited to her friend Lauren's thirteenth birthday party and was very excited to attend a big birthday party.

"Hi. Happy birthday! Are we the first guests?" I asked upon arrival.

"We only invited you and Allie," Jennifer, the party host mom, said.

Allie's attitude quickly changed into a scowl as she plopped down on the couch, disappointed that the party wasn't as big as she had assumed.

"OK, great!" I said, then I realized that I had misread the invitation. Allie proceeded to tell Jennifer, "This is a stupid party. This is boring." Then, she went into the kitchen and looked around for snacks.

I was taken aback by her nasty comments. "Allie, come in here, sit back down, and talk with us," I said.

"Can I have those cookies?" she half-asked, half-demanded.

"No, sweetie. Those are for another time," Jennifer said.

Allie was completely obsessed with the damn cookies in the kitchen, as she continued to ask for them. "Stupid dog. Go away," Allie sneered at their sweet dog that just wanted attention.

Against my better judgment, we continued our stay and sat down to play a board game.

"Yeah, I got more points!" the birthday girl cheered with sheer joy.

Allie then scowled, covered her ears, turned to her, and shouted, "You are too loud!"

I said apologetically, "I am so sorry, Jen. We can leave."

Jennifer, my dear friend, was so polite, even though we were both in the middle of a trainwreck. "No, no, please stay. It's okay, Joni." She insisted we stay.

I spent the next two solid hours trying to keep the peace with everyone involved. Mortified by my daughter's behavior, I did all I could to calm her down and resolve each of her irritations.

Sit down.

Be nice.

Don't say things like that, Allie!

I was an absolute mess because she was a mess. I became the mom that I never wanted to be.

At that point, my mind was a jumble, and I struggled to think clearly. It was finally time to depart and express my gratitude. I drove away defeated, exhausted, and completely embarrassed. What should have been a sweet birthday party for Lauren—one of the few friends Allie had—turned into a heartbreaking memory.

That afternoon, my emotions became worn out of all hope that her attitude and behaviors would ever get better.

I was hot.

I was bothered.

I am so sorry, dear friends.

Sick and tired. I was constantly in a battle of trying to get my teen to act nice and civil to others around her. It was a sinking feeling. Is this how the rest of my life—our lives—will be?

The day broke me. "This is the last straw of this fucking summer! I feel like giving up," I vented to Eric after we got home. He listened calmly while the cogs in his brain turned for a solution. He came up with a plan.

"Call or text me next time. I will help, Joni," he said.

That was it! I could use him as a lifeline.

He continued, "When the ship is sinking, Joni, and she's batshit out of control, you need to call me."

I appreciated hearing his words of solution in the chaotic situation. I often have a hard time thinking straight and finding solutions in the heat of the moment. I love this man.

My instructions were clear. Get me out of this mess! I'm going down fast, help! That was the plan, but unfortunately, it wasn't a full solution. We knew that. It was just a small tool for a bigger issue. She needed professional behavioral therapy. Again.

I learned a lot that summer, mostly because this special life requires constant tweaking and fine tuning. We all needed to get through the teenage years successfully and happily. In September 2018, the start of Allie's freshman year of high school, we started her third round of ABA therapy. It had been successful in the past, and we welcomed this much-needed lifeline to our struggles.

Therapy for Mom

My persistent worries and concerns over Allie's health began to take a toll on me, resulting in a steady increase in anxiety levels. Whenever Allie suffered a seizure cluster, my symptoms would worsen. Over time, I came to understand the close interconnection between my stress levels, anxiety, and digestive system. After thirteen years of experiencing constant stress and anxiety, I was diagnosed with generalized anxiety disorder (GAD) and post-traumatic stress disorder (PTSD). This diagnosis provided me with a greater understanding of the root causes behind my behavior and emotions and aided me with recovery and healing.

I chose to attend talk therapy sessions. My therapist taught me how to enhance my emotional regulation by teaching me how to recognize triggers which cause anxiety, and understand and express my emotions in healthier ways. She also helped me develop coping strategies when stressful events happen.

Self-care over the years has been such a buzzword, but I understand how important this is for me in my journey. Talk therapy sessions are just as important as reading, writing, projects, and socializing with friends to pull me out of a funk.

During a recent therapy session, she gave me assignment to "have more fun," as I need to focus on this out-of-practice area. I'm not sure how to go about reaching this goal, but it should be a fun assignment.

Perspective. Eric and I have an inside joke about it. For twenty years he has told me, in many different forms, I need a different

perspective. When my therapist brought this up to me, it was
laughable. I knew in that moment what he had been telling me for
years, and the joke is that I needed another human to tell me the
same thing. Sorry, honey! I love you.

Perspective is huge! If you can't change your surroundings or
conditions, then change the way you think about it. When Allie
is seizing, instead of taking on the energy of trying to stop the
unstoppable, I retrained my brain to understand that her body will
come out of it on its own. I cannot go into her brain and stop her
tonic-clonic. I instead tell myself: What can I oversee? I can help
her when she comes out of it with a smile. I can wipe her saliva
from her mouth, and give her a stuffed animal to hold. That is what
I can control.

Through the development of these coping strategies, I have
gained a more effective method to manage my stress, anxiety, and
PTSD symptoms. Although I am not completely free of my GAD,
I have learned to manage it by perspective-taking techniques and
deep breathing exercises.

4

A New Home in Cannabis Country

The summer of 2014 we left behind our deep roots in Minnesota and moved to Colorado to enjoy a more active outdoor life and pursue cannabis treatment for Allie's seizures.

When California legalized medical marijuana in 1996 with the passage of Proposition 215, also known as the Compassionate Use

The decision to move was a no-brainer.

Act, it became the first of many other states that soon followed. Colorado legalized marijuana on November 7, 2000, when 54 percent of the state's voters approved Amendment 20. This amendment to the Colorado state constitution allowed patients with certain medical conditions to use medical marijuana with a doctor's recommendation.

In 2013, there was a significant surge of interest in medical marijuana and cannabidiol (CBD) oil as news reports circulated about their potential for managing seizures among children. We followed the story of the Figi family who lived in Colorado Springs, Colorado, when we saw Dr. Sanjay Gupta's documentary *Weed*.

Charlotte Figi, a six-year-old girl with Dravet syndrome, had experienced over 300 grand mal seizures per week despite multiple pharmaceutical treatments when she began receiving doses of oil from a low-THC, high-CBD strain of cannabis. Charlotte's seizures dramatically decreased, and her story helped spread the word about medical marijuana, especially high-CBD strains. The Charlotte's Web strain of CBD oil, developed by the Stanley brothers, is a specific cultivar of hemp known for its high-CBD content and low THC levels. It played a significant role in popularizing the use of CBD as a medicinal supplement.

Sadly, in April 2020, Charlotte passed away but her legacy continues to positively impact many people.

The possibility of being able to gain control of Allie's seizures with cannabis filled us with complete astonishment and hope.

Our little family adjusted quickly to our new Colorado surroundings. Allie attended a local elementary school, while Eric and I dove deep into Cannabis 101. We quickly reached out to the community of like-minded individuals and met with professionals. With the guidance of her doctors, we started administering CBD oil to Allie, which we hoped would help control her seizures through natural means. This new chapter in our lives brought us a sense of hope that we had never felt before.

Eric and I created various oil concoctions. As a result of these efforts, we saw some improvement. Allie began to experience several months of seizure-free days versus having weekly seizures before taking the oil. She was maturing and her moods were stabilizing.

We celebrated and credited the benefits of the natural plant. While I absolutely love cannabis and all the seizure-free days it has given Allie, it did not cure them 100 percent. Maybe my expectations were too high to think she could be cured. I realized it was a mother's hope. I am grateful for our cannabis journey, and I will always be a huge advocate for its healing properties for the whole body.

An Internet Diagnosis

The ten years of not knowing why she was having seizures kept me up many nights. I was casting out and searching to no end for any clues.

The website's description of symptoms eerily lined up with Allie's.

We were negative on both sides for a family history of mental illness, chronic conditions, or any kind of seizure disorder. I was fishing in ponds of medical guesses, and mentally, I was running out of bait.

Around midnight one day in September of 2014, I sat on my bed and laptop illuminating my dark bedroom, going down the internet rabbit hole of pediatric epilepsy as I had done a thousand times before. But this particular time, I came across the PCDH19 Alliance website at PCDH19Info.org and in one paragraph I was introduced to PCDH19 epilepsy. Reading down the bullet points listing these symptoms:

- ADD/ADHD
- obsessions
- fine and gross motor deficits
- GI issues
- sleep disturbances
- autism
- anxiety
- hypotonia
- sensory integration issues
- normal development from infancy but with regression after seizure onset

My eyes widened and my heart pounded as I read with my mouth open. The website's description of symptoms eerily lined up with Allie's.

While reading, a small but specific trait stood out: these children loved swimming, and so did Allie, almost to the point of obsession for her. I had never heard about this specific type of epilepsy. Feeling excited and scared all at once, I told my husband, lying next to me, that everything on this site sounded just like Allie.

I went on Facebook to seek support groups that mentioned PCDH19 epilepsy. I found and messaged the support group hosted by the Alliance. The response back was heart stopping: "It sounds like your daughter has PCDH19 epilepsy. Have you ever had an epilepsy gene panel done for her to confirm?"

From that message on, our lives changed. *Finally,* our first solid clue, and it was a big one. My mind was racing. *Could all this be the result of a gene mutation? Could we get an answer from a simple blood test? And, WTF didn't her multiple neurologists over the years figure this out?*

It was more than I could understand. I found the one fishing pond I have been searching for so long. I had to get that epilepsy gene panel ordered for Allie.

At 4 a.m., exhausted after reading all I could about genetics and PCDH19 epilepsy, I collapsed into a deep sleep. I woke at 9 a.m. and called the neurology clinic. They directed me to the genetics department. I demanded the test to be ordered immediately, but nothing is immediate when you need it to be.

After many months of tirelessly navigating insurance coverage and juggling numerous neurology and genetics appointments, we finally succeeded in securing the much-anticipated epilepsy gene panel test. Allie's blood was taken and sent out to a lab. Then more waiting. Seven long weeks later, I received a phone call from our genetic counselor, Cindy, who confirmed my suspicion.

"Joni, you were right. She is positive for the PCDH19 gene mutation."

I sobbed in the middle of her chatter right after her words, *you were right.* After more than ten years of uncertainty and navigating through the relentless sea of search I finally received Allie's big diagnosis of *The Why.* Tears rained down my cheeks as I hung up the call that brought me enlightenment.

The symptoms of PCDH19 epilepsy can differ greatly, ranging from seizure severity and cognitive delays to other manifestations, all resulting from a mutation in the PCDH19 gene located on the X chromosome. Approximately 90 percent of individuals with a

PCDH19 mutation and epilepsy are female, while only a small percentage of males present with symptoms. Researchers are actively studying PCDH19-related epilepsy to better understand its genetic basis, inheritance patterns, and potential factors that influence the manifestation and severity of the disorder. There is much more research to be done.

For so many years, we'd had no idea it was a genetic mutation that was wreaking havoc on Allie. It slipped by multiple neurologists and epileptologists that studied her. When I confronted her neurologist with that question, I received a generic voicemail back that, "genetics were not necessarily tested back then." His weak answer frustrated me to my core. I understood genetics had still been in its infancy at the time, but the fact remains, her neurologist should have notified us that an epilepsy gene panel existed. From my research, I discovered the epilepsy gene panel was first offered to patients in 2012. It's designed to cover a wide range of genes associated with various types of epilepsy. It can detect genetic mutations or variations that may contribute to different forms of epilepsy.

The internet and social media connections provided me with that information and not our "trusted" educated doctors. I felt let down by a respected physician. But *le passé est le passé* (the past is the past.) I had to move forward and leave the anger behind.

A bittersweet feeling overwhelmed our family over the days that followed. While we were elated to receive a clear diagnosis, we were also heartbroken when we learned that there is no cure for our daughter's rare gene mutation.

Her medical treatments remained the same. She continued with the same pharmaceutical regimen. After all, it's just words on a piece of lab work paper; important words, no doubt. The fact remains, though, that Allie is who she is, which will never change.

I was grateful for the question that was finally answered after ten years of not knowing. Knowing changed me personally on the inside. A calm feeling entered my psyche as my motherly instincts were verified.

Although social media has its drawbacks, I prefer to focus on its positive aspects and utilize it as a tool for education within its support groups. Allie's was a social media diagnosis. And for that, I am grateful.

Seizure in the Bathtub from a Bath Bomb

Allie experiences overwhelming sensory issues when taking showers, so she chooses to take baths instead. Her love of bubble baths allows her to relax mentally and physically.

During one Christmas, Allie received a gift—a green eucalyptus bath bomb. Bath bombs are typically composed of baking soda, corn starch, citric acid, Epsom salts, almond oil, coloring, distilled water, and drops of essential oils for fragrance. After Allie climbed into the tub, I excitedly dropped the round bomb into her bathwater. Allie watched as it fizzed and released color. Within two minutes of dropping it, while the bath water was at maximum capacity, she had a tonic-clonic seizure. I held on to her convulsing body, making sure her head was above the

waterline, for over a minute until the seizure ended. I quickly
unplugged the bath stopper and called for Eric's help to assist. Out
of her ordinary pattern for a random seizure, my mind suspected
the bath bomb may have caused this one.

After researching essential oils, I learned there have been rare
reports of eucalyptus oil triggering seizures in some individuals
prone to them. My suspicions were validated more when she did
not cluster; it was a one-off episode. We now steer clear of bath
soaps and products that contain essential oils. Since making this
change, Allie has not experienced another seizure during a bath. I
learned to make bath bombs without adding any oils to ensure her
safety, and that has worked out well.

Seizure Types and Allie's EEGs

Epilepsy is a chronic condition marked by recurrent and
unprovoked seizures. Typically, a person is diagnosed with epilepsy
if they have had at least two seizures or a single seizure that
indicates a high probability of
future seizures. However, seizures   **I raise awareness
that occur due to known and   wherever I go.**
reversible medical conditions such
as alcohol withdrawal or extremely low blood sugar are not
classified as epilepsy. Despite producing studies, clues, and leads,
the latest medical journals have yet to find a cure for epilepsy.
However, two-thirds of all people who live with epilepsy can
control their seizures with AEDs. The remaining one-third have

what's called "drug-resistant" or "refractory" epilepsy and are not able to control their seizures with anti-epileptic medicines. That is Allie's case. No disrespect to medical doctors who study seizures, but I am frustrated at the fact that we are no closer to finding a cure for epilepsy than we were in 1912 when phenobarbital was prescribed for seizure control.

I am frequently asked, accompanied by a compassionate gaze, "Does she have grand mals?" If I had a dime for each time I was asked, I'd be writing from my luxurious beachfront property in Maui. I reply, "Occasionally. The medical community now refers to a grand mal as a tonic-clonic seizure."

This question used to bother me, but I'm no longer irritated. I'm more than OK with these innocent inquiries. I welcome questions, no matter how insignificant. After a decade of the "grand mal" question, my perspective has shifted. I take opportunities to raise awareness wherever I go.

Allie has three different types of seizures: absence, focal onset impaired awareness, and tonic-clonic. Allie's absence seizures cause a brief loss of consciousness that typically lasts just a few seconds. Although she shows few or no symptoms, it interrupts an activity, and she stares blankly. These seizures often start and end suddenly and can occur multiple times throughout the day. Allie's not aware of experiencing absence seizures, but she reports "lost time."

During the second type, complex partial seizures, now called focal onset impaired awareness seizures, Allie experiences brief, irregular jerks as her head turns to the right, lip smacks with right-side facial twitching, and inward curling of her right arm and hand.

She is not aware of the impairment, but she does fall into a deep sleep post seizure.

More than 50 percent of Allie's seizures are tonic-clonics. These are characterized by two distinct phases: the tonic phase and the clonic phase. She will experience severe ridged-muscle spasms throughout her entire body, which temporarily delay her breathing. Her face and lips turn blueish purple, making these seizures intense and potentially life-threatening; scary to watch. Lasting from thirty seconds to just under two minutes of convulsing, she comes out on her own. Her saliva pools up during and afterward and she automatically blows it out. We usually have a towel handy for any clean up. Unaware she's had one, confused and experiencing loss of speech, she enters a deep sleep of recovery. We recover too.

Seizures are captured and studied by an EEG, which stands for electroencephalogram, a non-invasive medical test that records the electrical activity of the brain using electrodes attached to the scalp. The electrodes detect and measure electrical impulses generated by the neurons (brain cells) as they communicate with each other. Sometimes this test is helpful for diagnosing and then determining the best treatment for seizures.

Over the past decade, Allie has undergone eight EEGs, resulting in zero successful seizure activity captures. Her AEDs must have been working well during those sessions. At two years old, Allie was due for her second EEG (her first one being at the hospital when she was sixteen months old). Cal, the EEG technician, was not only experienced with young children but also very kind during the EEG process. He applied twenty electrodes over Allie's scalp as we sat in a small office. Cal made Allie comfortable with pillows and stuffed animals as he instructed her to do various activities to help evoke brainwave patterns or trigger potential seizure activity. He instructed her to open and close her eyes, blow on a pinwheel, then stare at strobe lights flickering at various intervals. She enjoyed the fun activities. The "play" activity in her brain was recorded, and her doctor later studied the results. The process takes about an hour.

After the EEG is complete, the technician removes the electrodes from her scalp, then sends us to the bathroom to clean the sticky electrode glue from her hair with the combs, brushes, soap, and coconut oil they provide.

Another kind of EEG is called a twenty-four-hour ambulatory, which uses a portable EEG at-home device where she is free to go about normal activities while the EEG machine records her brain activity. Again, no seizures were captured.

If we wanted to capture one of Allie's seizures, her epileptologist would need to order an in-patient hospitalization, remove her anti-seizure medications, and wait for a seizure to be successfully recorded. We opted out of that option, but maybe someday we will take that route if we ever consider brain surgery.

What has successfully captured Allie's seizure is an external camera mounted on her bedroom wall. The SAMi Sleep Activity Monitor is a motion-detection alert system that uses video recordings to alert us when she is having seizures. More about the SAMi in my parenting tips later in the book.

Prosopagnosia: Forgetting the Familiar

One morning at a high school basketball tournament, Allie's former schoolteacher greeted her. "Oh, hi, Allie!"

"Who are you?" Allie asked.

"I am your teacher from last year. You know me!"

But Allie didn't remember her until she said she was Ms. Mary, who had taught her in seventh and eighth grade. If they had met in Ms. Mary's classroom with familiar surroundings, Allie would have recognized her. "Oh, I am sorry, my brain doesn't work sometimes," she explained.

I mentioned this to her epileptologist during a checkup. The doctor explained the neurological disorder called prosopagnosia, also known as face blindness. It affects Allie's ability to recognize and remember some faces. Part of her brain called the fusiform gyrus, which is responsible for processing facial information, is not working properly. This disorder may or may not have been caused by her seizures. Or she possibly could have been born with prosopagnosia; we do not know for certain.

"I'm like Dori, Mom," Allie says, relating to her forgetfulness through Dori, the lovable character from the movie *Finding Nemo*, who also deals with memory challenges. Although she can recall happy moments from her childhood, such as trips to the waterpark and other larger family vacations, she often forgets smaller events and encounters with people. Allie also struggles with understanding timelines. To help her, we use visual aids such as a thirty-day wall calendar and paper countdown rings for upcoming events. Recently she has mastered her iPhone calendar, which has been helpful for her to track upcoming occasions. I love technology!

VNS Therapy for Seizure Control

Allie's seizures became more frequent in her early teen years. She experienced fewer and fewer days between clusters and spent days in bed seizing followed by a long recovery time, her quality of life deteriorating. We opted to try a non-pharmacological treatment known as vagus nerve stimulation therapy or VNS. The Food and Drug Administration (FDA) approved VNS therapy for seizure management in 1997, and based on the available studies, information, and successful patient outcomes.

The treatment involved surgically implanting a device, the pulse generator, in the upper left chest area and a copper wire around the left vagus nerve in the neck. The device sends electrical pulses through the nerve that help to regulate the brain's abnormal electrical activity that causes her seizures. This treatment is sometimes referred to as a "pacemaker for the brain." Despite the intricate nature of the surgery and its accompanying risks, such as infection, pain, and bleeding, we remained hopeful.

On May 24, 2018, Allie was excited about her hospital visit for the procedure. To our surprise, she wanted to stay overnight, saying, "I love those hospital beds, Mom." However, an overnight stay wasn't necessary for this operation. An hour after she was wheeled into the sterile surgical room, she was in the recovery area. The doctors, nurses, and support staff were exceptional at Children's Hospital Colorado South Campus, Highlands Ranch. After a successful surgery and three hours from start to finish, we headed home.

Recovery was fast and without complications for our teen girl. She went through a seven-week adjustment period before we would see the effects of the VNS implant. Over the span of those weeks, Allie's doctor gradually raised the number of milliamps (mA) in the new device to a therapeutic level. At each "ramp-up" appointment, the device went up in increments of 0.25 mA via a consistent cycle of thirty seconds on followed by a five-minute rest. Allie's specific therapeutic mA level was 1.5 mA. During this process, her voice sounded like a vibrating strain against her vocal cords, like talking through a box fan, a side effect that was disclosed in our pre-surgery discussions.

At six months post-surgery, we noticed consistent benefits. Allie was having fewer seizures. Although we were noticing positive changes, we would have to wait an entire year post-surgery to evaluate her AEDs and decide if we could decrease any medications.

While the reduction in seizures was certainly welcomed, it came with an unfortunate rise in behavioral issues. Allie went back to self-harm by biting her arm and experiencing rage episodes, along with erratic mood swings. We tried our best to help her with therapy and calming strategies. A follow-up appointment with Allie's epileptologist confirmed our concerns. Common in patients with lifelong seizures and complications, her brain had somehow grown used to the electrical activity of her seizures, which she was now experiencing less of.

A year post-surgery, Allie's behaviors improved. We reduced one medication but not all. Although she wasn't completely seizure free, we were happy to see an overall improvement in her quality of life.

The VNS implant was a good choice and improved her active life for the better. The goal had been accomplished.

A Waterpark Seizure and Allie as the Teacher

Allie was now in her late teens and had a record of ninety-two days seizure free. We headed for a fun-filled weekend at Great Wolf Lodge Waterpark in Colorado Springs. It was a three-day weekend and busier than usual. Crowds of families with young children filled the hotel lobby waiting to get checked into their rooms. We ate dinner and quickly headed to the indoor waterpark before closing time. The energy level was high, as so many little kids were screaming in delight at the slides and activities it offered.

Allie and Eric went directly to the highest waterslide in the park to wait in a long line. The stairs were steep and looked like they touched the ceiling. Bingham and I found an area in the pool to shoot basketballs into hoops.

Suddenly, a dozen lifeguard whistles were blowing hard and long. A few lifeguards ran with equipment up the hundreds of stairs where Allie and Eric had headed just a short time before. My heart sank, and I knew in a second those whistles were for Allie. A mom knows.

I scooped Bing up, toweled us both off and waited for what I never wanted to see: Allie being carried down in a stretcher by two lifeguards. She was alive and appeared to be recovering from a seizure.

Eric's eyes met with mine across the busy pool and I knew without words what happened. Ninety-two days seizure free and bam, she had a tonic-clonic while waiting for their turn for the waterslide. Eric caught her before she crashed onto the hard metal stairs, then held her tight as she was seizing as a good Samaritan hurried to alert the nearest lifeguard.

I gathered our items then like a marching band followed Allie's stretcher to the back rooms of the waterpark. The lifeguards set her down in front of a tall open garage door. An ambulance and firetruck arrived quickly after. I assumed it was the resort's protocol to automatically call first responders in any emergency.

Her eyes were open, and she was smiling. "Hi, Mom."

I smiled back, as we have done thousands of times before. I said in a composed voice, "Hi, Allie, you had a seizure, and we are going home soon."

"Oh no, Mom, I want to stay and go on the slide." I knew she was confused and disappointed, but we couldn't stay, as another seizure could be looming.

While Eric and Bing left the lifeguard area to retrieve our belongings from the hotel room, the first responders finished assessing Allie.

One young lifeguard stuck close to us and filled out paperwork on his clipboard. My guess was he was around seventeen years old.

Tall and thin, his hands and fingers were shaking. His adrenaline must have been flowing at warp speed. I thought, *This young man got schooled in Allie's class tonight; I hope he's doing okay.*

"Ma'am, are you her mother?" he asked.

"Yes."

"OK, I have a few questions I need to ask you. What is her name and address?" Other questions followed until he completed his two-page form. He worked with us that night in a kind and professional manner. I never got his name, but I won't forget him and how he stayed with Allie. I'm pretty sure he won't forget us either.

Allie's life lessons are sprinkled here and there, in and out of people's lives, teaching them how sometimes the uncomfortable moments can be the best life lessons.

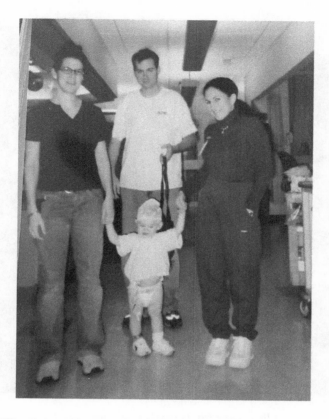

Allie, Eric, and me with a PICU nurse, December 6, 2004.
I don't know how I was smiling in this picture
as I was out of my mind and exhausted.

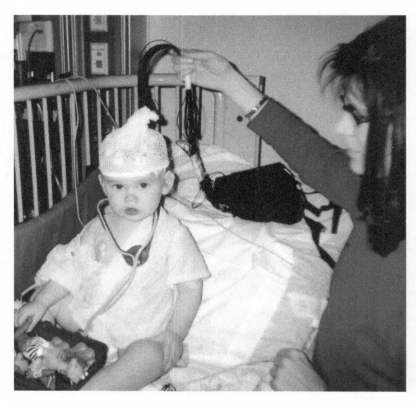

Allie in her PICU crib, December 7, 2004.

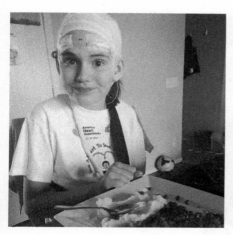

Allie wearing an EEG home monitor, 2014.

Allie repeated an EEG home monitor, 2016.

Allie and Bingham in a pile of leaves in our backyard Colorado, 2015.

Allie VNS surgery,
May 24, 2018

Allie recovering nicely
post-surgery, July 8, 2018

5
Don't Sing "Happy Birthday"

What makes people uncomfortable? Country, jazz, or rap music? A busy road? Dogs barking in the distance? A person singing completely out of tune?

On Allie's first birthday party at her nana's house, we joyfully sang "Happy Birthday" to her as she sat in front of a frosted pink cake. At just one year old, before her first seizure, she was already full of expression. Our daughter's infectious happiness filled the room, and we were in awe as she smashed the pink cake into her face.

The emotion she was feeling was called embarrassment!

During Allie's second birthday, now living with epilepsy, her surprisingly large vocabulary and unique personality were in full bloom. Again, we all loudly sang the famous song, but this time, I noticed she shielded her ears with her tiny hands until the song ended. Allie was extremely verbal; however, she was telling us something nonverbally.

At Allie's third birthday party, she gave us a huge clue into her growing mind. It was a sunny day at our home with friends and family enjoying the high energy of her special day. I leaned over my girl and lit three birthday candles in front of her with an audience surrounding us.

She calmly told me, "Don't sing 'Happy Birthday.'" No one else heard this request over the party noise. I was baffled by this request as I had never heard of a child not wanting the birthday song sung to them. The guests were waiting patiently for the start, naturally expecting this traditional song at a child's birthday party. I had no choice but to grant her request.

"Okay, everybody, Allie doesn't want us to sing the birthday song today, so she will make a wish and blow out her candles." I delivered the message with a high-pitched voice, excitement, and a smile. Was the high sensory input of background noise, people talking, and loud laughing too overwhelming for Allie? I asked myself.

From then on, Allie has been disturbed by the birthday song. She quickly covered her ears, squirmed, and made angry faces whenever the tune was sung at other children's birthday parties.

"It's okay, Allie. You don't have to be around when they sing," I told her one day during a larger party at our local recreation center. Allie, in her early teens, became physically agitated, her face was squished up in a fury, and her breaths were coming in huffs as she quickly darted for the door with me on her tail. We paced the hallway until the song was over and the cake was cut, then we returned to join in the celebration. I could see that her anxiety was gaining claws the older she got, as it turned into now physical agitation and was not healthy going forward. We needed to help her with these episodes before it grew out of control in other areas in her life.

"Why don't you like that song?" I asked her once.

Looking down with an intensely serious face, she replied in a growling tone, "It makes me feel uncomfortable. Everyone stares at me."

There it was! *That* was the solid answer I needed to hear. The emotion she was feeling was called embarrassment! I now understood after all these years. The song "Happy Birthday" triggered that feeling, and physical anxiety was the result. I understood embarrassment is a natural emotion we humans experience and an important feeling to have in certain moments. However, I saw the anxiety growing and gaining strength within her, which could at some point get out of control as she ages into adulthood. I knew a unique kind of therapy was called for.

Music therapy utilizes music to address various needs of individuals, such as emotional, cognitive, social, and physical needs. It involves working with a trained music therapist to listen to or create music, which can lead to improved mood, reduced stress and anxiety, and better overall well-being. A perfect fit to help Allie gain control. Kelsey, a trained music therapist, came to our home weekly for sixty-minute sessions. Together they sang and wrote music in fun playful activities while working to achieve specific goals. Allie's goals touched on emotional expression, stress reduction, communication, cognitive stimulation, motor skills development and social interaction.

I asked Kelsey for her opinion on Allie's avoidance of the infamous birthday song. She explained that it's not so much the tune or the words that upset her, because Allie enjoys music when she's in control. Some people don't like attention, and the "Happy Birthday" song is all about being the center of attention. Again, the answer Allie gave but with a deeper explanation.

I began to shift my thinking. It's possible that her discomfort can be traced back to early memories of being coerced into singing "Happy Birthday" without her consent, before we fully comprehended the complex sensory issues associated with autism. Something in her psyche would not let go of those deep-rooted, intense emotions.

We often evaluate other people's preferences and aversions through the lens of our own biases such as religious beliefs, medical choice, politics, science fiction, or unicorns; the list goes on. Allie is Allie. It doesn't make her a bad person because she loathes a song. I am certainly not going to make her listen to a song she doesn't enjoy, and I love her even more because of all her idiosyncrasies. They're what makes her so likable.

Allie has made significant progress in her goals from the times when she used to elope from the room with anxiety upon hearing that song. Today, she can stay in the room as the tune is sung to her friends while managing her emotions in a composed and mature manner. She clearly articulates yearly she doesn't want us to sing the birthday song on her birthday, and of course we respect that. I'm very proud of her maturity and growth.

6

The Snickers Confession

llie's first few weeks into the seventh-grade school year started strong. She was adjusting well (so I thought), and I greatly appreciated the care and attention provided by the teachers and staff at her middle school.

However, a few weeks after the school year started, Allie began adamantly expressing

Her confession came out in one breath.

her dislike for going to school. Middle school presented more challenging coursework in math, reading, and writing. "It wears me out, Mom," she told me during our morning commute.

"That's just what school is, Allie. You need to challenge your brain."

One early morning in November, while getting ready for school, I knew she had grabbed a piece of candy from her Halloween stash before leaving the house. I dropped her off at school and made the twenty-minute trip back home and began unloading the dishwasher. My phone rang, displaying "SSN Room" on the screen. School phone calls are unwelcome in mind with the first thought of Allie having a seizure.

"Hello?" I answered.

The special education teacher informed me that Allie had vomited and needed to be picked up.

"Okay, I'm on my way. Thank you," I said.

I wasn't too concerned because Allie rarely threw up, and I knew she was in good hands. For the next twenty minutes during my commute back, my thoughts raced as I tried to figure out the situation:

She doesn't want to go to school.

What made her throw up?

Could she have thrown up on purpose?

I entered the school and proceeded to the health office. The health aide looked at me in disgust and said, "Allie threw up on my shoes."

I turned my nose up from the stench and replied, "Oh, that is horrible! I am so sorry." I made sure to give some empathy.

Allie is very honest. She does not lie. Her confession came out in one breath. "Mom, I ate a Snickers so I would throw up so you would come and take me home."

I KNEW IT! I suspected somehow she did it on purpose.

"Snickers? Allie, you know better, it has peanuts in it," I said.

Allie's body had always rejected peanuts in any form—peanuts in shells, peanut butter, or peanut oil, her body simply couldn't tolerate them. The result was she would vomit. She knew about this. She figured out how to get sick and to be back at home.

We had discovered her intolerance when she was just one year old, and a teaspoon of peanut butter on her tongue resulted in a trip to the emergency room for the hives that subsequently covered her body. Fortunately, Benadryl took care of the issue within minutes. When Allie turned ten, she underwent a peanut challenge with her allergist and passed, allowing the doctor to declare her as non-anaphylactic to peanuts, meaning she was no longer at risk of going into anaphylactic shock and her throat would not close her throat if she ingested peanut.

Allie understood the intolerance and knew to ask if a cookie contained any peanuts. From an early age, she had always been very vocal about her allergy to everyone she encountered.

Snickergate was resolved with her swift confession to all in the room. The ride home was quiet, and she enjoyed a comfy day at home. Just what she planned. Later that night, I told Eric the story. We had a good laugh about it, and I thought about how smart Allie was to plan and execute a way to skip school.

Eric and I worked with her teacher to help Allie enjoy school through modifications of a work-play balance. The magic from teachers and staff made school enjoyable for her through her middle school years.

This episode was one of her most creative, defiant behaviors to date. I must give her credit. It may have to win some kind of award for being the best well-planned get-out-of-school trick. That takes some talent.

7
Balancing Marriage and Special-Needs Parenting

The years following Allie's first seizures were brutal on our marriage. An uncomfortable silence hung between us. Laughter, smiles, and simple kindness became void in our home. I was doing my best to survive as I juggled Allie's medical needs, medications, doctor, and therapy appointments, plus I buried myself in investigating why Allie's brain was broken. I was suffocating fast, never really taking the time to think or reflect.

We had to go through the dark before the light.

Eric and I were each unknowingly grieving in our own ways. My internal hatred of Allie's endless suffering was more than I could bear. I was mad at the world and bitter toward everyone. Loved ones closest to me became direct targets of my external rage, and slowly, it consumed my life emotionally and physically.

The person caught in the line of my fury was Eric. Each time Allie seized, it tore me apart inside, and I took my misery out on him. It seemed like he couldn't do anything right in my eyes. He was in constant defense as a result. He took more of a silent, cut-off approach when dealing with the chaos within our family walls.

Our marriage approached the brink of collapse. It became increasingly difficult for us to communicate in a healthy manner. Trying to fix my marriage was the least of my concerns and as a result, Eric and I grew further apart. We made the tough decision to sell our home in Saint Cloud, Minnesota, and move into separate apartments. We came to an agreement: Eric would take care of Allie most of the time at his apartment. That gave me a chance to take a much-needed break, allowing me to clear my head and figure out why our marriage was falling apart and the inner hell I was living in.

After much consideration, we decided to seek professional counseling and turned to Clara's House through CentraCare St. Cloud Hospital's partial hospitalization day program, a small counseling center located a few miles away. Since Allie was facing emotional and behavioral challenges that prevented her from attending school, Clara's House provided a day program and psychotherapy services to address her needs. With the help of intensive and collaborative therapeutic services, Allie became able to improve her emotional well-being and manage some behaviors.

Our therapist Julie, a licensed marriage and family therapist (LMFT), proved to be an invaluable resource and guided us through our marital issues that led us to our separation. Julie's expertise was particularly beneficial as she also worked with Allie in her day program and gained a deeper understanding of her needs.

Raising a child with extra needs had undoubtedly put a strain on our marriage; Eric and I acknowledged this during our couples therapy sessions, bringing the obvious that we buried so many times before into the light. Despite having considered the possibility of divorce, we instead both made a conscious effort to deeply commit to each other and our family for the long haul by choosing to support each other.

Over eight months, Eric and I started the slow process of repairing our broken marriage. Our special marriage had open wounds, but they have since healed. The emotions and exhaustion of parenting a child with Allie's condition has torn many couples apart permanently, but not us. We had to go through the dark before reaching the light. Looking back over twenty years of marriage, we both agree those eight months of separation made our marriage stronger. Eric is my best friend, and I enjoy being around him. I think he feels the same about me.

A Sibling's Role

A decade after Allie was born, we welcomed our second child, Bingham, or Bing for short. Our planned pregnancy went smoothly, and our baby boy was born in excellent health, bringing a sense of wholeness to our family. Allie had wanted a sibling for years, but with her medical complications, we needed to be certain we could give our second baby just as much love and attention as Allie. We did, happily.

In the first years of his life, I had inner questions.

Will her medical issues be too overwhelming for him?

How will he react at a young age to seeing Allie having violent seizures?

Will he be there for her when we are gone?

In his ninth year, those concerns disappeared as he showed natural maturity and compassion for his big sister.

According to a study done at the University of Illinois at Urbana-Champaign and published in the Journal of Intellectual Disability Research, siblings of children with special needs often develop greater empathy, patience, and tolerance than their peers who do not have siblings with special needs. They are also more likely to have a strong sense of responsibility, independence, and maturity. These siblings report feeling more positive emotions, such as compassion, toward others in their daily lives.

This study resonates with me as it aligns with Bing. He is the most empathetic, loving, caring son anyone could hope for.

As parents we need to pay extra attention and be aware for the well-being of all our children to make sure they're not living in the shadow of their brother or sister with special needs. These siblings have a greater responsibility compared to their peers.

They may have to take on additional responsibilities at home to help care for their brother or sister, such as:

- assisting with daily routines and help with tasks like food prep, dressing, or bathing.

- attend more doctor's appointments or therapy which can take up additional time and energy.

- be a role model or protector for their sibling, which can be a lot of pressure.

- miss out on typical childhood experiences or social activities because their sibling requires more attention or care.

Some siblings may feel like their own needs or concerns are not as important as their sibling with special needs. It could lead to feelings of resentment or frustration. We as parents have a bigger job to recognize and address the unique experiences and needs of all children, including celebrating their strengths and contributions to the family dynamic. Older siblings could be included in discussions about their neurodiverse sibling's care and treatment, and provided with opportunities for support and resources to help them navigate their own challenges.

Bonus! Siblings of children with special needs could also develop close bonds with their special-needs siblings and have a deep understanding of their needs and struggles. Bing has done so with Allie. I see him understanding that the world doesn't revolve around him, as there are bigger things around to be aware of. His incredibly compassionate, understanding nature toward Allie, and the traits that are shaping him into the person he is and will become, is truly a gift. And I don't take that for granted.

I Wouldn't Change a Thing?

"I love my little Timmy just as he is. I wouldn't change a thing."
Meanwhile, little Timmy is wreaking havoc in the classroom with the contents of a beanbag chair.

I have struggled personally with that phrase because I absolutely *would* change Allie's gene mutation in a heartbeat.

Allie remains the strongest person I know.

I feel a sadness deep down, grieve and cry about what she's been through and how different her life would have been if it wasn't for her multitude of medical issues.

I *am* thankful Allie is kind, caring, and full of empathy. I'm grateful that she doesn't feel pain during her seizures. And I often think about how lucky she is that she will never have to worry about big adult responsibilities that you and I deal with. She will always walk to the beat of her own drum; she will always shine in her own sunshine. Yes, she has medical challenges, but she has her own unique life and her own authentic joy.

One Last Word About My Unexpected Life

In Allie's first few years of seizures, my crying and self-loathing was a weekly occurrence. Now, in her adult years, I silently mourn less often for her and in different ways. I occasionally revisit my raw feelings of *What if she didn't have seizures?* These thoughts don't make me a bad person, they make me human. They help me release for a moment and then come back to reality. I'm allowed that.

I am constantly learning how to stay ahead of her needs, changes, and shifting requests of her new adulthood. I wonder what her future holds and what it will mean for our family as a whole. Despite my best efforts to plan ahead, I understand that unexpected changes can happen at any time, so I try to remain adaptable and open to new possibilities.

Allie's strength is nothing short of remarkable, especially considering the unimaginable challenges she faces every day living with complex medical issues, PCDH19 epilepsy, autism spectrum disorder, emotional dysregulation, obsessive-compulsive disorder (OCD), intellectual disability (ID), oppositional defiant disorder (ODD), sensory processing disorder, sleep disorder, excoriation disorder (skin picking), prosopagnosia (face blindness), and learning disabilities.

Yet despite it all, Allie remains the strongest person I know. Even when she's exhausted after a seizure filled day—a kind of exhaustion I will never truly comprehend—she never loses her life-force and lives each day to the fullest. Her fearless spirit takes her to enjoy the Colorado ski slopes with Eric. Then, to be immersed at the end of the day, she channels her creativity, self-tasked with the mission to craft beautiful pieces of art meant to place a smile on someone's face. And, if anyone knows Allie, she's got a great sense of humor—in fact, she's a very good joke teller. One of my favorites: What did one candle say to the other? Let's go out tonight!

PART TWO

Parenting Strategies and Tips

Introduction

In this second part, I provide a toolbox for your reference. It contains go-to advice based on my personal experiences of living and working the front lines of raising a child with special needs. What I have learned over the past twenty years is here at your fingertips in sort of a nutshell, a quick read for your own takeaway with solid advice and tips to help you navigate through challenging times, whether at school, socializing, or with an organization.

I understand you are busy, tired, and your time to read can be limited. I had that in mind when writing. This is a condensed version of my trials, errors, and wins parenting Allie. These are golden tips and strategies I wish I'd had so many years ago. And here they are for you my fellow super-caregivers. Some advice is for now and some for later when various issues arise.

Know you are not alone, as so many have walked this path before you and will continue after. Stay strong, my friend.

1

Welcome
to the Club

You and I are members of a collective group of caregivers and parents, bound together by a deep connection as we nurture and support our children with extra needs. We're an unspoken club that shares unique experiences that set us apart, including a shared language of disorders, medications, and treatments.

We understand our language and empathize like no other.

We are committed to a lifelong marathon. This special life is a part of who *you* are, to tackle an extraordinary loving mission. This colossal undertaking defines the very essence of parenting. While it can be chaotic, hard, and demanding, remember that you're not alone.

Unlike a broken bone that will heal on its own, our children's disorders, conditions, and syndromes are chronic and will not be cured. Many of us, like me, have logged over 10,000 hours in the area of special needs, without a degree printed out hanging on our office wall. We do it because we love: love our child, love being a parent.

There is an astounding wealth of knowledge that can be gained from other members of the club. We understand our language and empathize like no other. When you meet another like-minded parent, you will share a connection, union, and a sense of belonging because we *get it*.

Our struggles involve matters of life and death, and we cannot afford to look away. We are present with our children, ensuring they don't choke on their food, and take on tasks such as changing catheters and giving bed baths. We support each other as we navigate through our unique experiences and still have energy to offer advice and guidance. We celebrate every achievement, no matter how small, and share that common goal of improving our lives and the lives of our children.

Naively, I hadn't known this world existed. When Allie was born, I had expected to raise a healthy baby, then watch her grow up and leave the nest. To say the least, the depth of the community I've come to know and love in this life is extraordinary.

Now, let's get to work.

Short-Term Mindset

When you begin this journey, it's important to shift your mindset to the short term. Focus on immediate goals and outcomes rather than long-term plans or objectives. This shift involves prioritizing the immediate needs and tasks associated with the child's care and well-being, with less emphasis on future considerations. Temporarily setting aside your emotions can be helpful so you can approach a situation at hand with a clear and rational mindset to make sound decisions based on reason rather than feelings.

For example, when faced with decisions regarding your child's therapy, schooling, or new diet, the question to ask is, "What's best for my child right now?" Keep your child's quality of life as the foremost consideration in every new plan. When a therapist introduces a new treatment, they will explain and present the plan to you. Though it may sound like a fail-safe treatment, it may come with some challenges, such as scheduling issues, cost, and disruptions to your family and personal routine.

While these sacrifices are significant, remember that your child's quality of life is the ultimate priority. Instead of thinking this is forever mindset, view this new therapy as a temporary measure. Give it 100 percent of your effort, knowing it probably won't last forever. So, say yes to that extra therapy session and try it for a few months to see how it works. If it's not beneficial, then cancel and regroup. Eventually, everything will fall into place, and you will adapt to the new idea, overcoming any detours that may initially disrupt your personal plans.

2
Autism: To Tell or Not to Tell

The decision whether to tell the child about their autism diagnosis varies with each family and individual. It can even be somewhat controversial within a family. Some parents may be hesitant to label and tell their child they have autism and choose to refrain. As in the case of my old neighbor's son Kevin, who lives with autism without intellectual disabilities, whose parents chose not to tell him about his autism.

Whatever the choice is, the end goal is the same: to meet the child's needs and help them gain a better quality of life.

Kevin was diagnosed early on in his elementary school years unbeknownst to him. Because of his young age at the time, his parents were able to set up an IEP and monitor his behaviors to help him be successful in public school. But Kevin had difficulties making and maintaining friendships when he was young. He struggled with eye contact, had trouble understanding social cues, and his social advancement was slower than his witty younger brother's.

During his teenage years, he showed signs of low self-esteem, and his grades started to decline, putting him at risk of not graduating from high school. His parents put extra effort into supporting his needs, including hiring tutors. This paid off. Kevin graduated on time. He eventually got his driver's license and now holds a part-time job, lives on his own, and at twenty, started dating a coworker named Emma. Leading a fulfilling life, his confidence is noticeably improving.

How different would Kevin's life be if he knew about his autism diagnosis?

Will his parents ever tell him?

Is this fair to Kevin, not telling him?

Could there be a genetic component that is passed down to his offspring if he decides to have children?

Ethics are at the center of this discussion. Ultimately, Kevin's parents chose to take the path of strategic silence. Obviously, parents must consider the unique combinations of symptoms and medical issues of their individual child. To tell or not to tell, whatever the choice is, the end goal is the same: to meet the child's needs and help them gain a better quality of life.

On the flip side, to tell the child of their diagnosis they are in a better position to understand why they may feel, think, or behave differently than others. This understanding can help alleviate feelings of confusion or frustration. Also, they can better advocate for their own needs in various settings, like school or social situations. Knowing they have autism can help children find and connect with a community of others who have similar experiences, which gives them a sense of belonging. Finding comfort and friendships within the autism community is so beneficial!

Person-First vs. Disability-First

Can you see the difference between person-first vs. disability-first in these examples?

That downs lady Sheila works at the coffee shop.

vs.

Sheila, who lives with downs syndrome, works at the coffee shop.

Autistic Boy Builds World's Largest House of Cards

vs.

Boy with Autism Builds World's Largest House of Cards

Some media writers,

The bottom line is to be respectful.

content creators, journalists, and vloggers place the disability before the person. As a mother, advocate, and writer, I default to person-first language.

Person-first language emphasizes the individual before their disability, focusing on the person rather than their condition. For example, saying "a person with autism" and "an individual with disabilities" emphasizes their humanity and individuality above all else.

Disability-first language, also known as identity-first language, places the disability before the individual, emphasizing the disability as a vital part of the person's identity. Examples include "autistic person" or "disabled individual."

Some disabled people prefer using identity-first language (e.g., "autistic person" rather than "person with autism"), as they see their disability as an integral part of their identity. They don't wish to separate it from themselves. They may also argue that using person-first language can imply that a disability is something negative or something to be ashamed of, which is simply not the case.

Using person-first or identity-first language depends on individual preference. While acknowledging the disability is significant, it doesn't overshadow other aspects of the individual's identity. In other words, their disability doesn't define them. Their disability assumes a secondary role.

It's the Law

There are laws in place that examine the significance, impact, and preferences associated with these language choices, providing insights into respectful and inclusive communication practices.

In the United States, person-first language was written into law with the Americans with Disabilities Act (1990) and the Individuals with Disabilities Education Act (1997). The preference for person-first language versus identity-first language can vary depending on the specific community. For example, many in the Deaf and autism communities prefer identity-first language. However in writing, experts generally suggest defaulting to person-first language when writing about children, and generally using a mix of person-first and identity-first language when writing about adults or autistic individuals.

A Nod to Texas

In Texas, the legislature and the Texas Legislative Council are directed by law to use person-first language when enacting or revising statutes or resolutions. They are directed to avoid certain terms, such as "disabled," "mentally ill," "handicapped," etc., and replace them with person-first phrases like "persons with disabilities," "persons with mental illness," etc. They are also directed to avoid terms like "hearing impaired," "auditory impairment," and "speech impaired" in reference to a deaf or hard-of-hearing person, and to replace them with "deaf" or "hard of hearing," as appropriate.

The bottom line is to be respectful. In some cases, if you are comfortable asking, consider initiating a quick conversation with someone with disabilities to ask them what language they prefer when referring to their own disability. Some may not have a strong preference either way, but they may really appreciate your sincere attention, no matter what they prefer.

3
Advocate Up

This is a big one. You are your child's strongest advocate, and you need to own it. It's your responsibility to speak up on behalf of your child, as they may lack the ability to say, *Hey, something's not right.*

With our voice, we give them power.

Children with disabilities often face unique challenges that might be overlooked or misunderstood without a dedicated advocate. By advocating for a child's needs, parents like you and me guarantee that their child's rights are respected and that they receive an appropriate education tailored to their specific needs. Advocacy also plays a role in raising awareness and promoting inclusivity and understanding within the community. With our voice, we give them power. And that power is to advocate.

In school, advocacy ensures that the child receives all necessary supports and accommodations to facilitate their optimal learning and development. Do not assume that the school district catches everything.

Cathy, a member of my local support groups, is a mother to seven-year-old Jimmy, who has autism. She brought up a concern that he conveyed, "It feels like the words are jumbled up or mixed around when I try to read them. Sometimes the letters look weird or backward to me, and I get confused."

Cathy also mentioned to his teacher that Jimmy didn't show any progress in his reading skills by the end of his first school quarter and scheduled a meeting. Cathy met with the IEP team to discuss his lack of progress and asked for an evaluation to identify possible learning barriers. She also requested additional resources, such as more time on his IEP reading goals.

Cathy's advocacy paid off. The school assessments confirmed a diagnosis of dyslexia. With modifications to his reading instruction, Jimmy leveled up by the end of the school year. Cathy's advocacy was successful in advocating for Jimmy's educational needs and establishing a collaborative support system.

Advocacy Shows that Someone Is Looking Out for Them

Just like in other areas, advocacy in medication management is a huge task as well. We must voice our concerns when we observe that a medication isn't functioning effectively.

My child is crawling out of her skin and biting her arms this week. The only change was this new medication you prescribed. We need a change!

During challenging circumstances when a medication is wreaking havoc on your non-verbal child, speaking up for them is a must. The child doesn't have the vocabulary to explain why, what, or how they are feeling. Take a larger look at the bigger picture, such as what changes are recent. Any new supplements? New foods or dietary changes? Turn your brain into a personal detective for your loved one. It pays off! Speak up on their behalf because they need you to.

Advocacy is demanding and time-intensive work. While the rewards may seem intangible, your child's well-being is the ultimate prize, and for me, that is reward enough.

Tailoring Education

In the United States, the rules and regulations regarding IEPs fall under the Individuals with Disabilities Education Act (IDEA). IEP stands for Individualized Education Program, which is a legal document developed for students who are eligible for special education services. This federal law requires public schools to create an IEP for every student with a disability who meets the federal and state requirements for special education. The IEP helps ensure your child can access a free and appropriate public education (FAPE).

The IEP helps ensure your child can access a free and appropriate public education (FAPE).

The individualized learning plan is created by a team that includes educators, parents, and sometimes the student to help your child receive the support and services they need to succeed in school with the Least Restrictive Environment, or LRE, in mind, meaning students with disabilities should be educated with general education peers to the greatest extent appropriate.

The IEP outlines your child's strengths, weaknesses, and goals, and records the classroom and curriculum accommodations that will guide their learning. The goal is to provide a customized education that meets each student's unique needs. Your school district must annually review and update it to ensure it continues to meet the student's needs.

Special accommodations that can be included in a child's IEP vary based on the child's individual needs and challenges. Here are some examples of accommodations that could be included:

1. Sensory accommodations: can include noise-canceling headphones, fidget toys, or a sensory break area to help the child with sensory processing difficulties.

2. Communication accommodations: a communication device, visual schedules, or sign language instruction to support the child's communication abilities.

3. Academic accommodations: modified homework assignments, preferential seating, or extra time for completing tasks to support the child's academic progress.

4. Behavioral accommodations: a behavior intervention plan (BIP), social skills instruction, or a calming kit to support the child's emotional regulation and behavior.

5. Environmental accommodations: distraction-free testing areas, quiet spaces, or modifications to lighting or temperature to help the child's comfort.

If you're feeling unsure about IEPs, there is help. Seek out an expert in the field, called either a disability rights advocate or an IEP or education consultant, to help you through the IEP process. They are specifically trained professionals who keep current on those laws and regulations that affect special-needs children in our education system. Some of them charge fees, while others work for free or at a reduced rate.

We had mixed emotions about Allie's autism diagnosis at first. We quickly found that an official diagnosis from a psychologist helped her to not be expelled from school, as shared in a previous chapter. Getting a professional diagnosis from a doctor adds another layer of information to take into account when preparing an IEP.

The more I learned about the ins and outs of the IEP, the more I knew it served as an important tool for Allie. It's a much-needed document in supporting students with disabilities.

4

When Multiple Conditions Coexist

Comorbidity in medicine refers to the co-occurrence of one or more additional diseases or disorders alongside a primary disease or disorder. When counted as separate entities, comorbidities refer to each additional disorder or disease present. I mention this especially for anyone new to a first diagnosis to prepare you for the potential reality of additional diagnoses to

Epilepsy was not her only diagnosis.

follow. Comorbidities may require more frequent monitoring and follow-up appointments with healthcare providers throughout their lifetime.

For example, Allie's first official diagnosis was epilepsy at sixteen months. As she grew, her behaviors prompted further testing, leading to a series of additional diagnoses: ADHD, sensory processing disorder, obsessive-compulsive disorder, developmental and intellectual disorders, autism. Presented simultaneously, these diagnoses characterize a case of medical comorbidity.

While not a fun topic, understanding comorbidities can help you better navigate and manage your loved one's healthcare journey, making sure that they receive the necessary monitoring and support from healthcare professionals to maintain their well-being throughout their lives.

Country Club Doctor

Do you send undercooked, raw chicken back to the waiter and ask for a better meal? Of course!

What about at a doctor's office? Do you ever feel as if the doctor has rushed your fifteen-minute appointment? I call them country club doctors. This refers

High-quality medical care is not a luxury—it is your right.

to a doctor who embraces a "country club" lifestyle by working the fewest number of office hours possible to ensure they can promptly arrive at their 5:15 tee time at the country club, or whatever hobby they need to get to. Providing basic minimal care during brief fifteen-minute patient appointments creates low-quality attention.

It can be frustrating for patients who need more attention and care. Find a physician who prioritizes their patients and their well-being over their own pastimes. I've had my share! I have chosen not to return; I simply asked for a referral and moved on. This insight is not to insult doctors. Know that you have options if you're not satisfied with their bedside manner or service provided.

We have the right to quality healthcare. If you feel your doctor is not providing the care and attention you need, don't hesitate to seek out a new healthcare provider like I did. Find a doctor who will truly listen to your concerns and give you the time you need. High-quality medical care is not a luxury—it is your right. You should never feel rushed or dismissed by a doctor. Advocate for your loved one. Your child's health deserves full attention and expertise.

Medicine Management Doesn't Have to Be Mayhem

Regardless of the type of medication, be it AEDs, psychiatric meds, or cholesterol drugs, they all carry potential side effects that can disrupt your routine and manifest in various forms, such as weight fluctuations, headaches, dizziness, drowsiness, gastrointestinal problems, fever, or even severe psychological reactions like aggression, self-harm, hitting, and biting. The circus of various drug cocktails can go on for years while your child is prescribed different combinations until the right one benefits them.

Do not run out of medicine!

Medicine, pharmacy runs, and biomedical treatments are all important elements that will take up a lot of your time as a caregiver. It is a huge responsibility administering the necessary drugs to a child. It's no small feat and should not be taken lightly as it's a vital obligation that makes sure your loved one stays well and has fewer doctor and hospital visits.

Here are my tips on how to cope with the ever-important job of medication management.

Five Helpful Medication Management Tips

1. **Use a pill organizer**

    Life can be unpredictable. Staying organized is a must with meds. Confidently know which of your child's medications were administered or missed with a pill organizer. This handy tool can help you maintain organization, especially when more than one person is responsible for dispensing pills. If multiple doses are needed throughout the day, consider buying different colored pillboxes for specific times. For instance, you could use white pillboxes for morning doses and blue ones for nighttime.

2. **Plan ahead**

    Do not run out of medicine! Staying on top of this can be challenging, especially when traveling or during hospital stays. Plan for your child's doses and contact doctors or physicians well in advance.

    When obtaining a new prescription, inquire about prior authorizations right away to avoid delaying the prescription timeline. Keep in mind that the pharmacy may not have enough medication in stock, and it can take days to obtain after ordering,

particularly because deliveries aren't typically received
on weekends. Missing a dose could be a risk until
the pharmacy can restock. Lastly, consider holiday
hours when necessary to ensure you're prepared when
pharmacies and doctors' offices are
closed.

3.   Perform medication reviews

When your child is on multiple medications, be
sure to assess the necessity and effectiveness of the
regimen. The medication review process evaluates your
loved one's medication to ensure its safety, efficacy,
and appropriateness. This audit can be conducted
by healthcare professionals, such as pharmacists
or physicians, and could involve a comprehensive
review of all medications taken by a patient,
including prescription medications, over-the-counter
medications, vitamins, and dietary supplements. The
goal is to identify and resolve any potential drug-related
problems, such as drug interactions, adverse effects, or
inappropriate medication use. The frequency of these
assessments can vary depending on the child's specific
needs and the medications involved, but a good starting
point is to discuss this with your child's healthcare
provider. They can guide you on how often to evaluate
the medications and when to schedule medication
reviews.

4. **Don't be lazy about medication safety!**

   According to a study published in the Journal of Pediatrics, around 71,000 children visit emergency departments annually due to accidental medication poisonings, with 80 percent of these cases resulting from unsupervised intake. If you drop a pill, pick it up right away. Store them up high and out of reach. Do it every time and don't be lazy! You would feel awful if another child or a dog accidentally ingested pills because they looked like candy.

5. **Use a medication reminder app**

   Several medication reminder apps are available on smartphones, such as Medisafe, MyTherapy, Mango Health, and Round Health.

   Examples of useful features:

   - Set reminders for when to take medication.

   - Track medication adherence and dosage.

   - Store medication information, such as dosage and frequency.

   - Provide alerts for when a medication is running low or needs to be refilled.

- Connect with healthcare providers or pharmacies to manage prescriptions.

- Provide educational resources about medication and its side effects.

- Keep a record of medication history for reference during doctors appointments.

- Send notifications to designated family members or caregivers about missed doses.

- Offer customization options for scheduling reminders and dosage instructions.

5

Seven Things to Know: The Lessons I've Learned

Navigating the challenges and complexities of raising a child with special needs can

Things don't always go as planned.

be daunting. With that in mind, here are the top seven things that I wish I knew my first year of raising Allie.

1. **Repetitive paperwork**

    There seems to be a never-ending task of filling out medical paperwork for your child's various engagements and specialists, such as appointments, insurance, clubs, extracurricular activities, and hired helpers. This process may need to be repeated annually, potentially extending into adulthood. Specialty doctor appointments, in particular, may require filling out new forms for first-time visits. The task can become especially taxing when you're already coping with the stress and uncertainty surrounding a medical concern.

Utilizing technology to organize information can increase your efficiency. For example, scan and store your insurance cards in your smartphone. Scanning or taking snapshots of paperwork, legal forms, guardianship filings, and doctor's notes can help you access the information quickly and easily when you need it. Doing so will help save time and eliminate the need for physical storage.

2. **Get used to a revolving door of helpers**

    Do yourself a favor right from the start and get used to the ever-changing, revolving door of staff, helpers, professionals, respite care providers, doctors, and nurses in your child's life. It can be difficult to say goodbye to a therapist when they change careers or positions or move. You may have shared personal life events with the therapist and felt a bond, so be prepared for your family to feel a sense of loss when it's time to move on.

    Maybe you can relate to this scenario. Allie's music therapist, Ashley, with whom Allie had closely bonded for over two years, came up to me after a session.

    "Mrs. Brown, can I talk to you for a moment? I am taking a new position at a nursing home as their new activities director. I will miss all my music therapy clients, especially Allie."

Oh, great, I thought. The weight of breaking the news to Allie now fell to me to prepare her for Ashely no longer being in our lives.

This kind of change can be harder on the parent than the child in some cases! I made a point early on to be truthful with Allie about circumstances and not to shield her from change, but despite her taking the news well, I was disappointed about having to start over with a new music therapist.

3. **Review and adapt**

Embrace the ever-changing nature of your child's needs by regularly reevaluating therapies, school goals, friendships, and other aspects of their life. Micromanaging and advocating are never-ending when raising a child with special needs, even as they grow into adulthood. By keeping track and making necessary adjustments, you can avoid wasting time and money on ineffective approaches and therapies.

Take a look at this situation: After three months of speech therapy, six-year-old Hannah was still struggling with articulation and vocabulary. Recognizing the need for change, her mother, Kim, took the initiative to reevaluate the therapy.

She had a conversation with the speech therapist, asking important questions like, "Can we break down the goals into smaller, achievable steps? Are there alternative treatment options? Are you the best fit for Hannah?" The speech team responded positively and made small adjustments to support Hannah's needs. Hannah continued to progress toward her speech goals, and thanks to Kim's ability to advocate and adjust her daughter's therapy, she was able to prevent wasting time in hindering her daughter's development.

4.   **Be flexible**

Things don't always go as planned. While it can be stressful when things don't proceed as anticipated, the reality is most situations aren't a matter of life or death. Taking a mental step back and being flexible can help you adapt to new situations and make the most of unexpected opportunities. It can also help strengthen relationships by being open to compromise and understanding different perspectives. The ability to be more flexible can reduce anxiety levels and help maintain a sense of calm during uncertainty. In the next heated situation, take a deep breath, embrace the unexpected, and remember the benefits of being flexible.

5. **Know the limitations of your helpers' skills**

It can be difficult to rely on others when caring for a child with complex medical needs. Even if you have the strongest support team on your side, you are ultimately the one responsible for your child's care. And no one can take of your child like you can. Slightly lowering your expectations of respite helpers, nursing staff, family, and friends can help you avoid disappointment. For example, when hiring a sitter, expect adequate care, but do not to expect them to go above and beyond, such as guiding therapy exercises or administering complex medical treatments. Leave those areas to professional nurses or trained medical assistants. People have their own lives and problems to deal with, and our needs or requests may be too overwhelming for them to handle if we push them to their limit. There are always exceptions, as there are amazing, extraordinary people that come into our village and do go above and beyond. It may take time to find that special person, but when you do, keep them close and show your appreciation.

6. **Access help for yourself**

As a caregiver, know when you need help, and learn to feel comfortable asking for help. Family and friends are natural supports, but when dealing with complex issues, seek help from trained experts:

- Parent support groups

- Respite care providers

- Advocacy organizations

- Disability rights attorneys

- Educational consultants

- Special-needs financial planners

- Behavioral, occupational, speech, and physical therapists

- Hospital patient advocate

Let's take a closer look at respite care providers, who are individuals or organizations that offer temporary relief to caregivers of children and adults with special needs. Respite care offers services such as in-home care, day programs, community outings, and overnight care. This allows you to rest, recharge, and take care of your needs while ensuring that your loved one is receiving proper care and support.

Another expert worth examining more closely is the hospital patient advocate. Many people are unfamiliar with these skilled helpers. When your child is in the hospital you can request a patient advocate, a helping hand, if you will. These advocates often have their own department within the hospital, such as Child Life team, Patient Relations, Patient Support Services, or something similar. They provide support and guidance for you and your family, helping you navigate hospital matters, understand your rights, and access resources if needed. Their role is to help resolve issues or concerns related to your loved one's care and ensure that patients receive the best possible care. If you have traveled a long distance, they can provide information on nearby hotels or housing options. These hospital services can sometimes ease stressful situations so you can better concentrate on your child.

7. **Seek second and third opinions**

It's always a good idea to seek a second and third opinions with anything in life but especially for medical help. While your physician is knowledgeable, they may not have all the answers or meet your expectations. If you're feeling uncertain about a doctor, therapist, or staff, don't hesitate to seek alternatives. Although it may require extra time and effort, such as taking your child out of school for appointments or placing holds on their therapies, researching other options could be beneficial in the long run, especially if it results in meeting your child's needs more effectively.

6

Financial Course Altered

The financial burden faced by a family raising a child with special needs cannot be ignored. According to a study by the University of California, Davis, it can cost families an average of three times more to raise a child with autism compared to a neurotypical child. However, comprehending the full extent is impossible without firsthand experience.

It's common for young people to set a financial plan and goals for their future. Most have a plan in the back of their mind and want to figure out how to execute it. Eric and I had a plan to work hard, raise a family, travel, and comfortably retire.

Our world flipped upside down at Allie's first seizure. After that, we didn't think about the financial future; we just needed to get through the day. Our life plan and financial course was altered. Drastically.

I did everything humanly possible and medically safe to help Allie live a better and healthier life—and still do. There was no limit when it came to the amount I would spend to heal her. I spent money without blinking in hopes it would produce a magical cure. I purchased biomedical treatments, vitamins, specialty foods, homeopathic devices, oils, uninsured doctor visits, and labs that cost us our trivial spending.

The medical bills added up—nothing surprising there. In the first seven years, Allie's seizures were intense, and I found comfort in rushing her to the hospital for support. Opening medical bills from her previous hospital stay left me feeling stressed. To make matters worse, she often had multiple hospital visits in one month. We barely had time to unpack our bags before we were headed back for yet another admission.

One afternoon when I visited my neighbor Connie, whose daughter, Mazzie, also had seizures, casually mentioned using state waivers to help Mazzie get financial assistance for her medical bills and therapy services. Intrigued, I said, "Please, tell me more," as I was not well-versed with Medicaid. State waivers are programs that provide funding and services to families living with children who have special needs. They can help cover the costs of medical care, therapy, home modifications, and other necessary supports that may not be covered by your private insurance or other programs.

The range of services and waivers provided can differ from state to state. In Colorado, there are several Medicaid waiver programs available for individuals with intellectual and developmental disabilities. These programs offer a range of services and supports, such as home- and community-based services, respite care, and behavioral health services.

Here are some common services and items that Medicaid waivers may cover for children with special needs, although specific services and items covered can vary by state and by the child's individual needs:

- Assistive technology and devices (communication devices, hearing aids, wheelchairs)

- Home- and community-based services (respite care, personal care, skilled nursing)

- Behavioral health services (therapy, counseling, psychiatry)

- Prescription drugs and medical supplies

- Occupational, physical, and speech therapy

- Transportation to medical appointments

- Adaptive equipment and modifications to the home (wheelchair ramps, grab bars)

- Special education and related services (tutoring, occupational therapy, speech therapy)

The information was music to my ears—I was overjoyed to learn that there was financial assistance available for Allie's medical therapies and devices that she needed. I immediately rushed home from Connie's house and began filling out the paperwork.

I also want to recommend setting up a trust and will with a legal professional. A special-needs trust (SNT) is a legal arrangement designed for your loved ones with disabilities, allowing them to hold and manage assets while still qualifying for government benefits like Medicaid and Supplemental Security Income (SSI). Two main types of SNTs exist: first-party or self-settled SNTs, which are funded with their own assets and are typically created by the individual, their parents, guardian, or a court. Third-party SNTs are funded with assets belonging to someone else, like a parent or grandparent, and sometimes part of estate planning.

Before settling on an attorney for an SNT, which is a costly legal document, I suggest shopping around and consulting with an attorney specializing in this area of law to determine the suitability of an SNT for your situation, as they are a complex area of law.

7

The Mental Toll of Full-Time Caregiving

According to a study published in the *Journal of Intellectual Disability Research*, parents of children with intellectual disabilities show a higher prevalence of mental health problems compared to parents of typically developing children.

Take breaks: Yes, please!

The study found that 29 percent of mothers and 21 percent of fathers of children with intellectual disabilities had symptoms of anxiety or depression compared to 16 percent of mothers and 11 percent of fathers of typically developing children.

I didn't need a research study to tell me we have more stress and anxiety! Just talk to any parent. We can agree we are stressed, and sometimes it's a serious matter and not healthy on our bodies. When my daughter is in a seizure cluster, I am physically and mentally with her for her needs only. Self-care during that chaos

is just the basics: eating, breathing, and sleeping. There is no way
I can casually go to happy hour with friends or make a facial
appointment when life at home is hectic. When I can, I make sure
to get my self-care activities in order and executed to my benefit.

It's important for us to seek help and resources in managing
our mental health and well-being. Here are five steps to keep in
mind when you need to practice self-care:

1. **Establish a self-care routine**

   Get regular exercise, maintain a healthy diet, ensure
   adequate sleep, and set aside time for relaxation and
   activities you enjoy. You are doing yourself a favor by
   maintaining both physical and mental health.

2. **Seek support**

   This can be from support groups, therapists, friends, or
   family. Sharing your experiences and hearing about the
   experiences of others can provide a sense of community
   and understanding. Professional help, such as therapy
   or counseling, can help with strategies to deal with
   stress and improve your mental health.

3. **Take breaks**

   Yes, please! In your own time, of course. Allowing
   yourself to take pauses from your caregiving
   responsibilities can help you replenish your energy.
   Respite care or organizing for another person to help
   with caregiving duties is a win-win for your mental and
   physical health.

4. **Practice mindfulness and meditation**

    I know. . . buzzwords! Yikes. But doing so can help
    manage stress and anxiety and improve mental health.
    Read up on some techniques that can include deep
    breathing, yoga, or spending time in nature. We forget
    the basics of putting our mind, body, and spirit first and
    how important that truly is.

5. **Set boundaries and manage expectations**

    Say no! Understand that you can't do everything. Set
    realistic expectations for what you can achieve each
    day and learn to say no when you feel overwhelmed.
    Prioritize and let go of things that aren't pressing. This
    can help you avoid feelings of guilt or inadequacy, and
    maybe reduce stress.

A word of caution regarding relying too heavily on friends for
self-care. We all need a good friend to vent and let off steam to, but
most of our BFFs are not experts with degrees in the field of mental
health. While mental health was once stigmatized and considered
shameful, times have changed *(yippie!)*. Seeking professional help
for yourself takes incredible strength and courage, and your best
friend may fall short to take that on. Take care, my friends, but
don't burn out your BFFs.

Mental Exercise

What are your fears?

Do you fear uncertainty?

Do you experience high anxiety when your child is sick?

Do you fear death of a loved one?

For me, yes to all above. How can we reduce these valid thoughts and get them out of our head space?

Psychologists often observe that anger is a secondary emotion or a protective response to primary feelings such as fear, hurt, or sadness. Yup. I can relate. Anger is a cover-up for my underlying fear. It was always my go-to. My anger then flowed out onto my loved ones. I have been there too many

Aren't we already stressed-out mama bears?

times, and my family went down with me. My husband can attest to that, as he has been the first line of my discharged anger when Allie was in a seizure storm. My fears of her unwellness directly resulted in instant anger at whomever and wherever I gazed.

We give care to complex children, so it's natural to worry about their safety, and the mere thought of something bad happening to them can be unbearable. This is where anger lives. The aim is not to dwell in fear and anger. Instead, acknowledge when you feel it, then take steps to address your emotions so they don't overwhelm you or impact your daily life.

As caregivers, we need to acknowledge that our fearful thoughts can occasionally turn into a continuous, harmful flow.

While some fear can be beneficial in ensuring our safety, excessive fear can affect our mental well-being. It's Psychology 101, known as a negative feedback loop, where negative events or experiences trigger negative thoughts and emotions. Stop that cycle. It serves no purpose, period. Aren't we already stressed-out mama bears? Here is a quick mental exercise that helps me.

When experiencing a stressful problem, you can interrupt the spiral by asking yourself:

What is the worst-case scenario?

What would happen if that occurred?

Then, take a pause to recognize the thought pattern.

1. Interrupt the pattern: Once you become aware of the thought pattern, try to interrupt it by consciously shifting your focus. Engage in a different activity, such as taking a walk, doing some exercise, or engaging in a hobby. Physical movement can help redirect your attention away from the spiraling thoughts.

2. Challenge the thoughts: Examine the validity of the thoughts that are spiraling in your mind. Ask yourself if there is evidence to support them or if there are alternative perspectives. Looking at the thoughts rationally and challenging them can help break their hold over you.

This simple mental exercise is an invaluable tool that has helped me through my most intense situations and that I will continue to use.

Sleep

Make no mistake, we need to take sleep seriously to function in life, and it can be challenging for parents to monitor their children

Sleep well, my fellow warriors.

with nocturnal seizures. One solution can be to install a camera in the bedroom. A lot of parents keep their baby monitors for years just for that extra watchful eye at night.

The camera monitoring system we use to monitor Allie's nighttime seizures is the SAMi Sleep Activity Monitor, a nocturnal movement monitor. It utilizes two devices: the camera itself and an Apple iTouch. The latest SAMi software is downloaded to the monitoring app and connects to SAMi through local Wi-Fi, internet, or cell networks. The SAMi uses an infrared camera to capture any unusual movements during the night, then records the movements or episodes. You can save and play back all the recordings.

The camera is installed on the wall in Allie's bedroom, and the iTouch notifies us when she experiences a seizure. I can go anywhere in my house with my screen to monitor during the day.

No matter what camera system you use, it is a great solution for monitoring your child's sleep when you're asleep.

Our SAMi has recorded and saved hundreds of Allie's seizures. This footage proves invaluable when discussing her condition with medical professionals, and I am very grateful. Sleep well, my fellow warriors.

The Power of Community

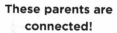

These parents are connected!

To whom do you turn for support and guidance? Family members can be helpful, but they might not always be able to offer the necessary assistance, as they have their own lives to manage. By establishing connections with external sources of support who can empathize with your experiences and connect you to helpful resources, you can create a strong support network that not only enhances your ability to navigate challenges but also provides emotional encouragement and practical guidance along your journey.

Here are some ideas to help you find support in your community.

- Seek out quality medical professionals: Your child's medical team, which includes doctors, therapists, and nurses, understands the medical component of your child's needs. However, you can go a step further with them by inquiring about additional resources they might recommend. They often have networks and unique connections related to specific medical diagnoses that could provide support, and some of these resources may even be located in your area.

- Join in-person support groups (a personal

favorite): Talking in person to another like-minded parent can provide a deeper connection and more meaningful conversations. These parents who are going through similar experiences can provide a sense of community which we all can benefit from. And as a bonus, these parents are connected! Some have been in your shoes and beyond.

- Join a Facebook support group: Some of the most intelligent parents I know are *not* on social media. I often urge them to explore this idea, or at a bare minimum, to only join specific groups and steer clear of the phony baloney. The online support groups can introduce you to events, information, and awareness about the special-needs community. Pretty much any chronic condition your child has, a group with a wealth of information exists, and you can access it without leaving your house.

- Seek out advocacy groups and organizations: This is how I found one of my best friends! Joyel Chambers is the director of Renew Respite, a nonprofit that provides free monthly care for children with special needs and their

siblings to support the caregivers by giving
them a night off while knowing that their
children are accepted and safe. I signed Allie
up and during my intake meeting, Joyel and I
instantly became friends.

- Other great examples include the Autism
Society, which provides support and resources
for individuals on the autism spectrum; the
National Down Syndrome Society (NDSS)
that advocates for individuals with Down
syndrome; and the Special Olympics, which
offers sports training and competitions for
individuals with intellectual disabilities. The
Council for Exceptional Children (CEC)
focuses on special education advocacy, and
Best Buddies International fosters friendships
and social inclusion.

Finding a support network requires seeking out resources
that will then snowball into natural connections with individuals,
resulting in friendships that last. They will provide the emotional
support you need. This will allow you to become the best possible
parent or caregiver for your child. The stronger your support
system, the better equipped you will be to face challenges and
navigate your child's unique journey.

8

Transitioning to Adulthood

The general goal for parents is to send their offspring into the world independently in hopes that they will live well and contribute to society in a productive and positive way. Of course! But it's a bit different for us. We want all of that for our loved ones, but we need to put more thought into navigating

We are in it for the long run until we die.

our young adults toward that goal. We must guide them with their living situation, financial security, food, healthcare, employment, and day programs.

This topic is huge and could be an entire book in itself. However, I wanted to address a few basic points to assist you in getting started navigating the transition to adulthood. Planning ahead could help alleviate future chaos and guide you with future preparation:

Guardianship or conservatorship: Setting up a legal guardianship or conservatorship for your loved one is highly recommended. Planning and having this in place early can be beneficial for both the child and their caregivers. There are three important benefits to establishing a guardianship:

1. Legal protection and decision-making: Parents or caregivers can continue to make important decisions on behalf of the young adult, ensuring their well-being and rights are safeguarded.

2. Continuity of care and support: The appointed guardian can coordinate with medical and support services, ensuring the loved one's needs are met effectively, leading to improved outcomes in health and education.

3. Protection from exploitation and abuse: Guardianship protects them from potential harm by providing a legally authorized guardian who acts in their best interests, minimizing the risk of exploitation and ensuring their safety.

Government benefits: Familiarize yourself with government programs such as Medicaid, Social Security Disability Insurance (SSDI), and Supplemental Security Income (SSI). These can be valuable financial sources of support for your young adult. The process may be lengthy at times, but it is undoubtedly worthwhile to implement it for the long term.

Professional advice: To help you navigate legal, financial, and social systems, seek advice from professionals like special-needs attorneys, financial planners, and social workers.

Draft a letter of intent: This is sometimes referred to as a family letter, which outlines your wishes and expectations for your child's care. Include detailed information about their daily routine, medical history, likes and dislikes, as well as any other special instructions.

Establish a special-needs trust: Doing so helps ensure your child's financial stability. A special-needs trust is designed to manage resources for a person with a disability while maintaining their eligibility for public benefits.

Take out life insurance: Taking out a life insurance policy with the trust as a beneficiary can add a layer of financial help for them after you're gone.

Arrange for future caregivers: Who are potential caregivers? Think about siblings, family friends, or professional caregivers who can step in when you're no longer able. Make sure these individuals are willing and able to take on and sustain responsibility.

Perform regular reviews: Regularly review and update your plan to ensure it continues to meet your child's changing needs and circumstances. Laws and regulations also change over time, so make sure your plans are still in compliance.

This is a process of continuously adapting and making decisions that best serve your child's well-being. If you have already begun, commend yourself for your foresight. However, if you find yourself as a late planner or a procrastinator, it's okay. Begin the planning process as soon as possible, allowing ample time for legal, financial, and care planning, and the flexibility to adjust plans as circumstances change.

Remember, this is our marathon. We are in it for the long run until we die.

My Reflections to You, My Village

As parents of children with extra needs, we are committed to a lifelong marathon, witnessing and celebrating every achievement no matter how small. My expectations of raising my healthy baby Allie and watching her grow up living her life freely

I'm never stepping out of this war zone.

was anticipated; I would have never entered this special world if it hadn't been for her. Naively, I didn't know this world of such strong, courageous parents and caregivers existed. The depth of this community I've come to know and love is extraordinary to say the least. We share a common goal of improving our lives and the lives of our loved ones, and for that, I am grateful.

My family—Eric, Allie, and Bingham—are the driving force behind my transformation, having shaped me into the person I am today. I have evolved into a pretty kick-ass caregiver, mother, and wife, and have gained extensive knowledge and insights into this extra-special life.

I will never give up on Allie. I have a passion and a drive to win her daily medical battles, while knowing full well I'm never stepping out of this war zone. Forever, no matter how exhausted I am, and for the deep love of my Allie, I will accept the challenges and continue full steam ahead. Writing this book has provided me with time for reflection, comfort, and calmness. I can confidently say, wholly and truthfully, what a beautiful purpose I have.

Thankful

Thank you to my immediate family Eric, Allie, and Bingham. Without their support, I cannot breathe, and my love for them is beyond words.

To Grandma Marge, my sweet mother who visits often from Minnesota and laughs with her grandchildren when she flies into town. We "hit the ground running" and she happily keeps up with our chaos.

To my late father Larry, a resilient, smart, self-taught man who rose from the challenges as a young boy in the harshest childhood environment anyone could imagine.

To Nana, even though she is thousands of miles away, her FaceTime sessions with Allie are so meaningful and helpful all year.

To Grandpa Dennis, fellow author, for sharing FaceTime jokes with Allie and always picking up when she calls.

To Jolene and Jodi, my sisters, who know when I call I need to talk now.

To Aaron, the best uncle Allie and Bing could ever want.

To my nephew Jaimie, a strong role model to Allie and Bing and who will continue to be a part our lives in a positive way.

To Joshua and Jacob, sorry for the pee incident in your toddler pool! Allie loves her cousins.

To my Aunt Pat, we have beautiful memories in her backyard pool.

To my Aunt Joan, like a second mom and who has walked this special path before me.

To Joyel Chambers and Anna Burriesci, who are there unconditionally for the best and the absolute worst of my days.

To the Youngquists, you all have seen our family go through so many transformations and gave laughter and support through it all!

To Jody Froeschle, you were there in the beginning dear friend and saw it all.

To Kelly Hume-Hodges, who said, "Let's write together!" at Witches Tea so long ago.

To Charlotte and Roxy Peterson, our bond of friendship formed instantaneously.

To Mary Caricato, Mesa Middle School SSN teacher, and staff Sheila, Libby, Carla, Stephanie, and Michelle, who always went above and beyond. Remarkable people who touched our lives for the positive.

To Nicole Jones, Castle View High School teacher, who taught Allie at so many levels, elementary through transition program, from childhood into adulthood and rose to the challenge each and every time.

To the PCDH19 Alliance and friends, not just a support group but a survival group for me. Julie Walters, Karen Wells-Kilpatrick,

Dana Massey, Heather Fryman, April Haganey, Sophie Meskis, Jennifer Holland, Julie Wismann, Christy Rollins, Bart Kilpatrick, Matt McManus, Jody Warshawsky, and Helen Owen, who have touched so many lives and provide knowledge to a community that is bound by a special life.

To the principal at Weaver Lake Elementary who in her last year before retirement ran after Allie when she eloped out the elementary school doors and around the building as I pulled up. I am so sorry, but wow, what a trooper you were! I really should have remembered your name.

Resources

PCDH19 Alliance to learn more about PCDH19 epilepsy and get connected to a community of support. www.PCDH19Info.org

The ARC a national organization that supports individuals with intellectual and developmental disabilities as well as their families. www.TheArc.org

The Chelsea Hutchison Foundation a nonprofit corporation formed to provide help and support to individuals, particularly children and young adults, who have epilepsy. ChelseaHutchisonfoundation.org

The SAMi Sleep Activity Monitor a motion detection alert system that uses video recordings to alert us when she is having a seizure. www.samialert.com

About
the Author

Joni Brown is the youngest of three
sisters and grew up in Eagan,
Minnesota, a suburb twenty minutes
south of the Twin Cities, Minneapolis and
St. Paul. Her parents divorced before she
turned three.

As a child, Joni had great memories
of her father, Larry, who often took her
and her two sisters camping to various
Minnesota state parks. Joni also enjoyed when her mother, Marge,
took them to visit the family farm in Pine Creek, Wisconsin. It
was there that Joni learned the old-fashioned values of hard work
paying off, including processing beef and deer with her uncle,
Larky Losinski, and harvesting apples and hickory nuts. She
admired the strong academic traits of her grandmother, Gladys
Schank, and her great-aunt, Helen Losinski, both schoolteachers,
and her great-aunt Blanche Losinski, who was a school principal
and advocated for children with learning disabilities.

Joni graduated from Saint Cloud State University (SCSU).
During her time at SCSU, Joni and Eric met and married in 1999.
They started a family in 2003, and currently reside in Colorado.
This is Joni's first book. Visit Joni-Brown.com.

Together We Carry On

On days when seizures come to call,
I part the curtains, let light fall.
I wash her face and brush her hair,
Though we won't be leaving her bedroom's lair.
Tears may fall, though I try to be strong.
These days seem endless, arduous, and long.
As we stay within this quiet space,
I ponder life's fleeting, transient pace.
These hours give time for reflection
On both her struggles and my own afflictions.
But we carry on, through joy and strife,
Navigating this journey called life.

https://linktr.ee/jonibrownauthor

Printed in the USA
CPSIA information can be obtained
at www.ICGtesting.com
LVHW091959140124
768653LV00009B/464